EMOTIONAL IMPACTS OF LIFE BEYOND CONVENT WALLS

EMBRACING NEW HORIZONS

ADAKU HELEN OGBUJI, CCVI, PhD

En Route Books and Media, LLC
Saint Louis, MO

ENROUTE
Make the time

En Route Books and Media, LLC
5705 Rhodes Avenue
St. Louis, MO 63109

Contact us at
contactus@enroutebooksandmedia.com

Cover Credit: Sebastian Mahfood

ISBN-13: 979-8-88870-540-7
Library of Congress Control Number:
2026940486

Dedication

This work is dedicated to all former religious individuals who are seeking fulfillment on their faith journey.

Acknowledgements

This book could not have been finished without God's unwavering love and indispensable blessings. I thank God for guiding me through every step.

I am thankful to my Congregation Leader, Sr. Celeste Trahan and her Leadership Team and all the Sisters of Charity of the Incarnate Word of Houston, Texas, for their prayers and support.

My mother, Fidelia Lucy Ogbuji, and my siblings, Fr. Udo, Gloria, Henry, and Prisca, are wonderful to me. I thank them for their warm love and inspiration. I cherish the gentle love of my late father, Joseph Ogbuji, who gave me love and taught me how to care for others in love. The love of my nephews, Chigozie, Akachukwu, Enyioma, Chimdike, Gerald, Greg, and my niece, Amarachi, has added a special flavor to my life, and I'm grateful to them.

My relatives and friends accompanied me on this journey, and I sincerely thank them. I am grateful to my cousin Joy, my sister-in-law Nkiru, Uncle Austin Igbuku, Sir Pius Ogiji, Fr. Dr. Reginald Temu, Fr. Dr. Emmanuel Foro, SJ, and Sr. Dr. Anne Arabome, SSS.

I also appreciate En Route Books and Media, especially Dr. Sebastian Mahfood, OP, for publishing this work. You all mean a lot to me; thank you!

Finally, I am grateful to all the individuals who generously shared their stories and participated in the extensive research that made this book possible. I am especially thankful to the 110 religious women and 50 former religious women who were interviewed during this process. Since the list of those who contributed to this work is long, I carry your names not just in ink but forever in my grateful heart. I pray that God rewards you with His peace and favor.

Table of Contents

Chapter One

Introduction

Between June 2016 and October 2023, I met several former Catholic sisters (ex-nuns) who were struggling with depression and unhappiness after leaving the convent. Some were hesitant to share their stories due to a lack of trust, while others were afraid to revisit their unhealed wounds. Many of these individuals feel helpless in their current situation and are unable to function appropriately in civil society. Some blame their former congregation for their struggles, while others have joined a new congregation but still struggle with pain every day. While some still hold on to bitterness and continue to wear the veils and emblems of their former religious congregations in the pretense that they are still in religious life, others are happy with their new life outside of religious congregations. Unfortunately, some individuals have even contemplated suicide when faced with departing from religious life.

From the stories gathered during this exploratory work, it was obvious that some former religious individuals were traumatized, confused, bitter, and in great psychological need. Some claimed they were unjustly asked to leave the convent, while others deliberately asked for a year out from the congregation and never returned. In contrast, others claimed they were dismissed without following the proper procedures outlined in their Constitutions or the Canon Law. Many are still searching for another congregation that will accept them back to the convent. Why is the decision to leave the convent or be dismissed from religious life sometimes followed by a critical moment of anger, sadness, confusion, trauma-related feelings like depression, or relief in some cases?

Ex-religious Person # 1 expressed during the interview:

> "Before being dismissed from the convent, my formator made life difficult for me, calling me names and threatening that I would be kicked out during evaluation/assessment. This caused me to live in fear. At times, I felt

intense anger at the way I was treated but couldn't confide in anyone. I endured the oppression and cruel behavior silently, suppressing my emotions. At some point, I felt bewildered, depressed, and traumatized, leading to illness. Then, the formator told me one morning that the letter for my dismissal had been sent to her by the leaders since I was not happy in the convent and was always sick. When I left, my life was in shambles. I felt despair, rejection, and hopelessness, wondering if I would ever be normal. I felt as if God had abandoned me. I avoided going to church because I didn't want to be reminded of the terrible experience. I also refrained from talking to anyone out of fear of being ridiculed or embarrassed. I spent most of my time in bed, lacking appetite and struggling with sleeplessness. When I began school, I found it challenging to concentrate. It took me over two years to overcome my excessive fear and lack of trust in God and the people around me."

Psychological distress, such as anxiety or fear-based symptoms, as expressed by ex-religious # 1, may occur after exposure to a traumatic or stressful event. The DSM-5-TR may classify the trauma experienced by ex-religious person #1 as an adjustment disorder or an acute stress disorder (APA, 2022, pp. 319-320). Adjustment disorder refers to an intense reaction to a stressful change or event that is more severe than what would normally be anticipated. This can lead to difficulties in interacting with others, as well as in the workplace or school. The symptoms of this disorder include feelings of sadness and hopelessness, frequent crying, anxiety, sleep disturbances, reduced appetite, poor concentration, and social withdrawal. Rachel M. Daly (2020), writing from New York, told her story in *Homiletic and Pastoral Review*:

> "In the fall of 2014, I got on a train to enter the convent. I was happy and healthy, with an intact family, great friends, a list of accomplishments I was proud of, and no history of mental health trouble, having passed my psychological evaluation with scarcely a blip.

Ten months later, I discerned to leave. I reentered the world anguished and spiritually disoriented, with almost no clothes, no phone, no computer, no money, no prospects, and most of my relationships in a state of serious disruption. I hoped that within a year or so, I would be back to my old self, but it wasn't to be. I spent the next not one, not two, but three years battling anxiety and depression. I struggled to find a job. I would have spells of nausea and faintness that would send me to the couch for hours at a time. For long stretches, I was unable to go a day without crying."[1]

One of Daly's respondents, Phillipa Martyr, expressed:

"Wonderful article, speaking as an ex-temporary professed, (I left an enclosed order in late 2007). I know that I and other ex-members of religious communities have usually carried a heavy burden of shame and of feeling – and

---

[1] https://www.hprweb.com/2020/01/pastoral-care-of-women-who-have-left-the-convent/

> being made to feel – like a complete failure. This is partly caused by some religious houses' ways of forming people, e.g., 'If you have a vocation and you leave, you will never be truly happy again' (yes, this is an actual quote from my experience). But it's also partly caused by the perceptions of the community you return to: the too-proud parents who now have to explain to everyone that you're back, the friends who moved on because they assumed you were gone for good. And, of course, the judges and juries who decide you were too weak, too sinful, too flawed, too crazy, too sane, too fat, too thin, too old, too young, too beautiful, too ugly, too smart, too dumb, too whatever to 'succeed' in the vocation to which you felt called."[2]

Many ex-religious men and women have shared stories about the significant and traumatic impact of leaving the convent. During this research, when asked whether they were receiving counseling help,

[2] https://www.hprweb.com/2020/ 01/pastoral-care-of-women-who-have-left-the-convent/

some former religious individuals mentioned that they couldn't afford counseling, while others didn't believe they needed it. In contrast, others admitted they had talked with a few friends or their spiritual directors yet remained in shambles. Leonie's Longing, a non-profit organization, created to serve the needs of women who have been in the convent or monastery and returned to lay life, puts it well: "When a woman exits religious life, she typically only has the clothes on her back and a few personal items. Quite often, she goes home and stays with family or friends while she discerns her next steps. The first needs are physical – clothes, food, housing, transportation, etc. After these are met, she has emotional and spiritual needs. For example, can she get a ride to Mass? Can she find a spiritual director? Does she need a good counselor? Returning to lay life is another stage in a woman's life journey. It can be confusing and exciting. The noise of life in the secular world contrasts sharply with the quiet honorarium in the convent/monastery."[3]

[3] https://leonieslonging.org/

The recognition of trauma-related experience among former nuns/sisters has highlighted the necessity for further research into how religious congregations dismiss their members, as well as how to offer psychological support for individuals who have left the convent and are coping with the challenges of life outside the walls of the convent. This book is possible through the wealth of data gathered from many leaders of diverse congregations, formators, active religious members, who are neither leaders nor formators, and a good number of former consecrated religious women. The experiences and stories used in this work are composites of the 160 participants who responded to the questionnaires and interviews conducted. A simple random sampling technique was used to select 30 different congregations of women. The focus area was not disclosed to ensure the participants' privacy. The participants come from diverse cultures, including Africa, Asia, Europe, and North and South America. The participants comprised thirty consecrated persons in leadership ministry (Group 1), thirty formators (Group 2), fifty religious who are neither leaders nor formators (Group 3), and fifty former consecrated religious (Group 4) who made first or perpetual vows before leaving the convent.

Sampled Congregation Number	Group 1 Leaders	Group 2 Formators	Group 3 Active Religious	Group 4 Discontinued Religious	Total Participants
30 Congregations	30 Sisters	30 Sisters	50 Sisters	50 Ex-religious	160

As a consecrated religious involved in a formation ministry, I chose not to interview any former members or consecrated individuals from my congregation to avoid any potential conflicts of interest. I initially felt hesitant and unsure about conducting this research because I was uncertain about my moral obligations in doing so. However, I understand the importance of doing what is right, taking responsibility for my actions, learning from my mistakes, and striving to become better. I am only a work in progress!

Of the 110 who participated in this work in groups 1 to 3, 93 are perpetually professed sisters, and only 17 are in temporal vows. All the participants in groups 1 and 2 have made perpetual vows. Thirty-three participants in group 3 have made perpetual vows, and 17 are in temporal vows. This figure suggests that participants in this work are highly mature in their religious life, having lived longer in their respective religious institutes.

The thirty leaders in Group One held various leadership positions, including community leaders, regional or provincial leaders, and general councilors. The thirty formators in Group Two serve in various formation ministries, including vocation animators, postulant directors, novice directors, directors for sisters in annual vows, and formation directors. The control group consists of fifty participants in group three who are neither formators nor in leadership ministry. This group was crucial as the leaders and formators were protective of their congregations when answering specific questions. This control group was unbiased, and the data collected from them in all the questions provided insights into their respective religious congregations. The data from the leaders, formators, and sisters in the control group was collected using a questionnaire.

For the fifty dismissed religious, the interview method was used to gather data. Of the 50 participants, 20 were interviewed via phone because they were unavailable, and 30 respondents were interviewed face-to-face. The snowball sampling method was used to identify individuals to be interviewed. This method involved interviewing individuals, who then provided contact information for other former religious individuals to be interviewed. The majority of the fifty dismissed religious who were interviewed left or were discontinued during their annual vows (thirty-one participants), while the rest left or were discontinued as perpetually professed sisters (nineteen participants).

This figure suggests that the majority of respondents were dismissed within the first nine years of their religious formation. This raises questions about what may be happening in religious formation houses. These individuals (sisters in annual vows) are at the initial stage of formation and at the mercy of their formators. Sometimes, their ability to make perpetual vows depends on how much they respect, obey, serve, and almost "reverence" their formators.

On the other hand, the dismissal of a perpetually professed religious person is more complicated and sometimes requires a dispensation from the Holy See (pontifical congregations) or the local bishop (non-pontifical congregations) if the person has committed a grave offense.

The research was conducted between 2016 and 2023, and the participants, who demonstrated immense courage, allowed me to share their stories in this study to convey their experiences of leaving the convent and the psychological trauma that they suffered. However, their names and congregations were not mentioned to protect their privacy. When participants are quoted, their actual words are used but sometimes edited for clarity and anonymity.

Some religious men experience similar challenges. However, this work specifically examines the experiences of religious women, as the majority of those affected, emotionally wounded, and still retaining and wearing the habits of their former institutes are mostly former consecrated women. Due to this limitation, this work cannot be considered the total experience of all religious people. Another limitation is the profound emotional struggle, fear, shame, and lack of trust some dismissed religious individuals exhibited during the interview. The participants initially had difficulty sharing their experiences with the researcher. However, once the researcher assured them of confidentiality and listened to them with respect, unconditional positive regard, and empathy, they became more open. In fact, some interview sessions became therapeutic, and as a result, additional free therapy sessions were arranged.

The researcher faced resistance from former religious individuals. Seven ex-religious persons initially agreed to be interviewed, but they canceled on the day of the interview, expressing inability, unwillingness, and sudden anger in opening the wound. Another challenge was locating these former religious; sometimes, those who had their phone numbers were hesitant to give them out. When a telephone interview was conducted due to the participant's unavailability, the researcher did not have the opportunity to explore non-verbal communication and emotions that are not easily conveyed over the phone. Due to the trust that was established, many former members of religious institutes requested therapy sessions. The researcher was only able to provide free therapy sessions to a couple of them and directed the others where to get help.

Apart from these limitations and challenges, the work concisely explores the process of dismissal in thirty different congregations, the impacts of dismissal on former consecrated religious persons, and how they can cope with life after the convent. This research work is crucial in shedding light on these issues and advocating for the support and understanding of dismissed religious women. The book also aims to empower women who may be victims of religious trauma syndrome (Winell, 2007, p. 2) and provide them with insights and the skills to cope with life beyond the convent. Building upon existing knowledge and discoveries in the field of mental health, the book offers insights into psychospiritual studies that aim to help and empower individuals who are wounded by their experiences with religious life or have left it.

This work is grounded in Aaron Beck's (1983) cognitive theory and Winell's (2007) concept of Religious Trauma Syndrome (RTS).

Beck's theory examines how information processing influences human behavior and the process of behavior change. According to Judith Beck (2011), the cognitive model posits that dysfunctional thinking is common to all psychological disturbances, and when people learn to evaluate their thinking more realistically and adaptively, they experience improvements in their emotional state and behavior (p. 3). Cognitive theory is crucial in this study, as it explains how negative thoughts and beliefs can lead to dysfunctional cognitions and behavior. For instance, if people's beliefs are distorted and negatively influenced, it can lead to difficulties in coping with life. These beliefs can influence an individual's core values, making them more susceptible to future challenges and hindering their ability to cope with stress. For former religious individuals, negative cognition and belief can make it challenging to live a fulfilled life outside the confines of the convent.

On the other hand, Winell's Religious Trauma Syndrome (RTS) illustrates how leaving a religious community can be traumatic. She compares this trauma to the experiences of loss, such as death or divorce, which can bring feelings of anger, resentment, emptiness, despair, isolation, and sadness. The concept of religious trauma syndrome is vital in this work because it sheds light on how leaving religious life can lead to psychological issues for some former sisters/nuns. It also highlights the intense stress, sadness, and confusion that can accompany the process of grieving the departure from religious life.

Significance of the Study Area

The relationship between psychological trauma and leaving religious life is a significant concern for many families and religious members, yet it is an area that is rarely discussed. The inclusion in the DSM-IV of a new diagnostic category, "Religious or Spiritual Problem," marks a significant breakthrough. For the first time, there is acknowledgment of distressing religious and spiritual experiences as non-pathological problems. The Diagnostic and Statistical Manual-Fourth Edition (APA, 1994) defines Religious or Spiritual Problems in Code V62.89, as follows: "This category can be used when the focus of clinical attention is a religious or spiritual problem. Examples include distressing experiences that involve loss or questioning of faith, problems associated with conversion to a new faith, or questioning of other spiritual values which may not necessarily be related to an organized church or religious institution" (American Psychiatric Association, 1994, p. 685). Religious and spiritual problems are so essential to mental health that this code was also added to the new edition of DSM-5 (APA, 2013, p. 725), and later to DSM-5-TR (2022 code Z65.8, p. 834).

This book is significant because:

— It gives voice to the psycho-spiritual trauma experienced by many former members of religious institutions. It explores the maladjustment and inappropriate coping behaviors among those who have left religious life, which has become a concern for the church and society members (The Kenya Conference of Catholic Bishops, 2014).

— This work may assist former religious individuals in processing the trauma of leaving the convent and acquiring coping skills to function effectively in society.

— This work will hopefully assist religious congregations in evaluating their dismissal process and the support they provide to their former members.
— The Formators, who accompany the candidates, may better understand the candidates by acquiring appropriate formation skills, which may help them work out suitable approaches to helping and guiding formees/formandis to psychological maturity and development opportunities.
— The Major Superiors or Congregation Leaders and their council members may be helped to patiently navigate the dismissal process and gather all the necessary information before the process is completed.
— Families of dismissed religious members may benefit from the study and learn to support their daughters.
— Individuals who are not consecrated religious will also benefit from the study by gaining insights into how they can handle their crisis of faith to prevent maladaptive behavior.

This work is limited, as it focuses only on consecrated religious women and may not represent the experiences of religious men who have been dismissed from their institutes. Hopefully, this exploratory work will assist many wounded former religious individuals in reintegrating into society after leaving the convent. The next chapter will explore the identity of a religious person and the process of discernment for those considering a life of celibate consecration.

Chapter Two

Formation Process in Religious Life

Consecrated life is an extension of our baptismal commitment. It offers a vast spectrum of options for those "men and women who, obedient to the Father's call and the prompting of the Spirit, have chosen this special way of following Christ, to devote themselves to Him with an 'undivided' heart. Like the Apostles, they too have left everything behind to be with Christ and put themselves, as He did, at the service of God and their brothers and sisters." (Pope John Paul II, *Vita Consecrata* #1). It is a life where being celibate, poor, and obedient is not a misery but a joy and a life of self-giving love. It is a life focused entirely on imitating Christ and lived within the Church. The activities of every religious institute are guided by the spirit of the founder, the charism, spirituality, constitutions, the individual charism of the members, and ultimately, the Gospel values.

A religious institute or religious congregation, according to Canon Law, is a society in which members pronounce public vows, either perpetual or temporary, which are to be renewed when the period has elapsed, and who lead a life of brothers or sisters in common (Can. 607, § 2). Each religious institute strives to demonstrate God's love in the world through community living and to lead a religious life in imitation of Jesus Christ, according to the unique way of life of each congregation. Individuals belonging to these religious institutes are commonly referred to as religious persons or consecrated celibate persons. It is in the community that a religious person lives out the religious vows with joyful service devoted to the church and its members. That is why Pope Francis encourages religious persons to wear a smile in order to humanize the communities.

He expressed: "Since we are witnesses of communion beyond our vision and our limits, we are called to wear God's smile. Community is the first and most believable gospel that we can preach. We are asked to humanize our community and build friendship and love. Our monastery or convent must not be a Purgatory, but a family. There will be problems, but, like in a family, with love, we search for a solution. We should not engage in unhealthy competition, but rather build community life with a big heart that lets go of grudges. We are called to be patient with everything and everyone and smile from our hearts. It is a sign of joy!"

Living in the community can be challenging, and Pope Francis is aware of the difficulties of community life. He explained: "From experience, I know that community life is not always easy, but it is a providential training ground for the heart. It is unrealistic not to expect conflicts; misunderstandings will arise, and they must be faced. Despite such difficulties, it is in community life that we are called to grow in mercy, forbearance, and perfect charity" (Pope Francis' address to Religious Communities in Korea on August 16, 2014).

A religious person is, therefore, one who is consecrated by the profession of the evangelical counsels of poverty, chastity, and obedience, and who follows Christ more closely through the guidance of the Holy Spirit. They are dedicated to God, whom they love above all, for the purpose of building up the Church and the salvation of the world (St. Ignatius, 2002, p. 390). Schneiders (2013) compares religious life to the parable of the Hidden Treasure and the Pearl, narrated by Jesus in Matthew 13:44. According to her, religious life is like a treasure that a person finds hidden in a field, out of joy, sells all they have to buy that field (p. 1). Religious life, as an institution in the Catholic Church, can be traced back to the first century. The Catechism of the Catholic Church comments: "From the very beginning of the Church, there were men and women who set out to follow Christ with greater liberty and to imitate him more closely by practicing the evangelical counsels. They led lives dedicated to God, each in their own way" (CCC # 918).

Religious life manifests in the Church as a beautiful marriage brought about by God with religious persons, who, with their whole existence, serve God in love through serving humanity (St. Ignatius, 390; can. 573, § 1; Vatican II, 2014). However, in order to become a religious person, one must undergo an initial formation process to adequately prepare for this way of life under the guidance of a formator. The formator must be adequately trained for formation ministry to guide formees in initial formation. Such preparation would assist them in expanding their self-knowledge and discerning the inner dispositions and attitudes of those in formation to avoid causing harm to the formee (Ogbuji, 2024). Maganya (2016), an African priest, also agreed that formation has to be holistic and cater to the psychological, spiritual, theological, moral, anthropological, and sexual dimensions of human development. Thus, well-trained personnel are needed in formation houses (p. 143). The individual continues to be formed until she makes perpetual vows; this is regarded as ongoing formation.

It is unfortunate that some formators are not adequately prepared before they are sent to the formation house. All the participants in this project—leaders, formators, sisters, and former religious—were asked: **Do you agree that your formators are properly prepared for the ministry? Please explain.** Twenty-one leaders agreed that their formators were well-prepared, while nine leaders indicated that some of their formators were not adequately prepared for formation ministry. Below are some of their responses:

- Yes, some of our formators are adequately prepared, but some did not receive in-depth training. We faced a challenge in replacing a former formator. Unfortunately, an untrained sister was sent to take her place. She ended up staying in the formation house for many years without receiving proper formation training. (Eleven participants expressed this concern).
- Some formators are adequately prepared, while others are not. In my congregation, a retired teacher was asked to temporarily replace a formator. However, she has stayed in the formation house for many years, and still does to this day. This is unfair to the formandis, who are treated like her students.
- Most formators are trained, but they need regular updates. Some have been in formation houses for over twenty years and still use the same old method, which may not work in this modern time, where those joining religious life have access to so much information.

- Some formators are assigned to formation houses based on their connections with leaders, while others are assigned for their introverted and prayerful nature. Formators require proper training (4 participants expressed this concern).
- Most of them are trained, but some are not well-trained, and they are sent to formation houses because they are available and seem to be living a balanced religious life.

Among the 30 formators interviewed, 22 participants agreed to some degree that they were properly trained, while eight formators admitted that they were not appropriately trained for formation ministry. Below are some of their responses:

- I was sent to the formation house without any training, and I struggled, especially at the beginning. I wish I could have been sent to the formation program (4 participants stated this concern).

- I was not adequately trained. I was a teacher, but was asked to be a formator because I was available.
- Some formators are properly prepared, while others are not adequately trained. When I was sent to the formation house, I hadn't received any proper preparation; however, I am now undergoing training. I made a lot of mistakes, and I wish I had received this training from the beginning.
- I only have a certificate in counseling and lack in-depth training in formation, human psychology, and development.

Of the 50 sisters who are neither leaders nor formators, 27 admitted that their formators were not adequately prepared, while 23 affirmed that their formators were well prepared for the ministry. Below are some of their responses:

- Yes, they are adequately prepared, but some of them lack moral competence.

- Yes and no, some are trained and efficient, some are not, and they cause chaos in formation houses.
- Yes, most of them are adequately prepared, but it is not only about the training. Some see themselves as "gods."
- Yes and no. I have confronted our leaders for involving untrained members in the formation ministry. It's very frustrating for the unprepared formators (2 participants).
- Some are not adequately trained. My formator was a teacher. She often felt frustrated because of the ministry, and the formees lived in fear because we were treated as her students (6 participants).
- To an extent, yes, they are prepared. However, some formators appeared to lack emotional maturity, allowing their personality and past hurt experiences to impact their ministry. Some may need emotional healing (7 participants).
- Formation is the work of the Holy Spirit, but some formators mistakenly think it is their work. They need to be well-informed.

- Some formators are trained catechists, some are teachers, and others seem to be prayerful. They are sent to the formation ministry without proper preparation in human and psychological development. Formators need to be adequately formed before they can be sent to the formation ministry.

The data collected indicate that many formators are adequately trained and missioned for formation ministry, while some are not. Nine leaders explained how unprepared sisters struggled in formation ministry, while eight formators confirmed that they were not well-trained, posing a big challenge in their various formation houses. Is it not proper to sufficiently prepare formators spiritually, psychologically, emotionally, and theologically so that formandis can experience sound growth and maturity in their formation process? Sometimes, when formators are not adequately prepared, it creates a crisis for both the individual seeking guidance and the formator who is unsure of how to help and accompany the formees. Thus, formators require appropriate training before they are assigned to work in formation ministry.

Gitau (2016), Ezeani (2007), and Maganya (2016) criticized the practice of assigning a member to a formation ministry without proper preparation. They emphasized the importance of adequately preparing formators, as they are involved in the personal lives of those they are forming. When formators are not formed, their self-confidence is affected. They sometimes feel threatened and insecure when dealing with more learned formees. As a result, various measures are employed to punish the formee, including dismissal. This scenario is not healthy for either the vulnerable formator or the formees/formandis. The inadequate training of some formators may confirm what Ezeani explained: "Some formees are unjustly dismissed from religious life when the formator's stand is challenged."

Ex-religious # 5 expressed: "My formator was not actually trained; she was a teacher. She used to assert her authority over us and treated us like slaves. Her words were considered absolute laws that had to be followed, so we couldn't suggest anything. Anyone who dared to speak up and offer suggestions was seen as disobedient and not showing the appropriate level of respect for the vow of obedience. Those who wore masks were considered to be good sisters."

Ex-religious # 24 explained: "During my formation years, my formator accused me of being pompous and arrogant because I didn't agree with some of her perceptions about certain events. She often focused on my mechanical engineering degree and seemed envious because she only had a high school certificate. The leaders dismissed me without giving me a chance to explain myself. I've moved on since then, but I strongly feel that the way some former religious persons were treated was unchristian."

Adequate preparation will help formators expand their self-knowledge and understand the rapidly changing and developing world governed by high technology. This will ensure that the formation process is holistic and comprehensive, addressing the psychological, emotional, spiritual, theological, moral, anthropological, and sexual aspects of the individuals undergoing the formation process. When this is not the case, it affects both the formator and those being formed. Today's youth have access to a wealth of information; some may be better informed than their formators. It calls for much humility on the part of the formator and to stay updated on what is happening in our world. At this age and time, it is challenging for young people to consider the call to religious life. Thus, those who arrive at our doors to discern God's call to religious vocation should be treated with respect, love, and support as they prayerfully discern whether God is calling them to religious life. Smith (2017) concurs: "Many religious congregations work hard to get young women to join them. However, the manner in which some members are separated from the convent can be disturbing in its suddenness and mystery." Some religious congregations are coming to completion/fulfillment due to a lack of new candidates. Those blessed to have young discerners are to nurture their faith rather than scare them away.

Apart from being adequately prepared intellectually, formators must also address their past wounds and insecurities. Simply going through a formation program or having a degree in theology and psychology isn't enough. It's essential to consider the healing of the emotional wounds that we all carry. When we neglect to address our emotional wounds through spiritual direction and psychotherapy/counseling, we may unintentionally harm the vulnerable individuals who remind us of our own shortcomings and shadows, or with whom we have a personality conflict. Some of the former religious individuals interviewed expressed how the wounds of their formators manifested:

Ex-religious # 14: "My formator acted like a 'god,' and her words were set in stone. She treated me unkindly, calling me names and making life unbearable. She frequently compared me to other formees and constantly sought out my mistakes, finding fault in everything I did. She would gladly share my mistakes with the entire community members, like singing off-key during prayer or setting the silverware incorrectly at the dinner table. I constantly lived in fear of what she might say or do next. Her lack of education led to very low self-confidence, and she felt threatened of forming a master's degree sister. She convinced the leaders to dismiss me because she believed that I had problems with the vow of obedience. I was angry and suffered emotional trauma. But now, I am recovering because I am going through psychotherapy sessions."

Ex-religious # 6 explained: "I think I had a personality clash with my former formator. She seemed to dislike me for no reason and treated everyone else with kindness. Sometimes, she would buy gifts for the members of the community and give them the gifts in my presence to make me feel bad. She frequently reminded me of my poor and difficult upbringing, making me feel inferior, insecure, and afraid."

Ex-religious # 35: "I was sexually abused by my formator. She threatened to send me home if I told anyone. I endured this for a long time, feeling fearful, self-pitying, and blaming myself until I finally found the courage to leave the convent. I was afraid to seek help from a counselor, even though I really needed it. This burden is becoming heavier every day. You are the first person I am confiding in."

Christina M. Sorrentino (2022) also narrated her abuse: "I could not believe that the same women who first welcomed me with beaming smiles and open arms could treat me with such wickedness and coldness... It was over the course of a little more than two years that, gradually, more and more each day, the tension continuously built up between my novice director and me. There was a constant fear and anxiety that enveloped my being due to a never-ending verbal, psychological, and emotional beating that I received from someone who was supposed to be my "spiritual mother." Many times, I would tremble during the Holy Sacrifice of the Mass, knowing that she was waiting to "pounce." If the flame of a candle was not high enough, if I dared to fulfill a priest's request as to how to set up the sacred vessels or vestments different from how we were trained to set them up, if Father wanted a Votive Mass instead of the Mass that Sister chose for the morning, or if he gave a homily she did not like, I knew I would face her wrath. When I was cleaning up after Mass, I would see her come in and close the sacristy door, and I learned the barrage of insults was coming my way... Bruised, battered, and broken from my experience, religious life became a living hell for me, and the best version of myself began to disappear with every scourging that I received from my tormentor… Each day, as my novice mistress vehemently berated, belittled, mocked, and gaslighted me, I daily offered up my suffering to Christ and for the sanctification of Catholic priests, as I knew that it was a gift that enabled me to become closer and closer to Him. I could not bring myself to surrender my vocation, and I continued to tolerate the abuse up until the last day when I left the convent."[4]

Formators, like all humans, are also wounded. Hiding in the guise of religious life will not save them from their wounds. In my book, *"Influence of Childhood Experience in Faith Development: A Journey Toward Wholeness,"* I explained how, in a formation house, a new candidate was asked to say grace before meals. When she began with "Hail Mary," the formator shouted at her and told her not to mention the name of that "woman" again. The formee was shocked and flabbergasted, wondering why the formator was afraid to hear the name of Mary, Mother of Jesus (Ogbuji, 2019). We won't be able to help others if we aren't healed ourselves. When we

---

[4] https://www.missiodeicatholic.org/p/behind-the-convent-walls

undergo a healing process, we become "wounded healers" (Henri Nouwen). It's important to remember that one of the positive aspects of going through difficult times is that as we receive healing, we also learn how to help others heal. St. Paul puts it well in 2 Cor. 1:3-4: "Blessed be the God and Father of our Lord Jesus Christ, the Father of compassion and the God of all comfort, who comforts us in all our troubles, so that we can comfort those in any trouble with the same comfort we have received from God." A healed formator is more compassionate, patient, open-minded, and loving; and even when it is crucial and necessary to terminate a candidate, it will be done with kindness and much respect for the person's dignity.

How does a religious congregation initiate and dismiss members during their initial stages of formation? Is there sufficient support for them after the dismissal process is completed? What causes some dismissed religious individuals to accept their situation positively and move on, while others struggle to cope with life? The following chapter will examine the procedure for dismissing members from religious congregations.

Chapter Three

Separation Process from Religious Life

The call to religious life and the response to this call are gifts from God. When Jesus says, "You did not choose me, I chose you" (Jn. 15:16), that means we didn't choose ourselves. God calls us and gives us the grace to respond: "Here I am, Lord, send me" (Is. 6:8). Everyone has a vocation! Some are called to the priesthood, others to married life, and others to religious or single life. Sometimes, we play God by telling candidates that they don't have a vocation. Candidates may not be chosen to join a specific religious community, but that doesn't mean they don't have a vocation. It's a matter of "many are called, but a few are chosen" (Mt. 22:14). In fact, it is difficult to know precisely whether God is indeed calling us to a particular congregation. That is why the process of discernment is very crucial and necessary (1 Sam. 3:1-11).

As a consecrated religious person, sometimes I think that God must be "out of His mind" to choose me to be a religious. Like Jonah, I postponed the call for a long time. I wanted to "find a boat" and escape this life (Jonah 1:1-17). But all my efforts were fruitless. Even though a fish did not swallow me up to bring me to a consecrated celibate life, God still found a way to get me back. Thus, despite my "late response," I see myself as unworthy of this call. However, I know that God's grace is sufficient for me, for His power is made perfect in weakness (2 Cor. 12:9).

When discerners leave everything to join religious life, it can be challenging to persuade someone who is completely certain that God is calling them to religious life that they may not have a calling to that specific congregation's charism and spirituality. For instance, if a candidate seeks entrance to a religious institute of apostolic life and always prefers to be in the chapel praying, this lifestyle is contrary to the active apostolic life. Therefore, the said candidate will be more comfortable in a contemplative order where her charism will flourish. If a candidate has a gift for teaching, she will be naturally inclined to join communities with teaching apostolates that align with her gifts. This is why the formation process is crucial in religious life, as it enables the candidate and formators to discern together to determine what is best for the candidate. Can. 661 explains: "Throughout their lives, religious are to diligently continue their spiritual, doctrinal, and practical formation. Superiors, moreover, are to provide them with the resources and time for this." This continuous formation helps a religious person develop a deeper faith and become spiritually and emotionally grounded to live a fully religious life in union with the Person of Christ (Ogbuji, 2019).

There are times when it becomes clear that a person considering a religious vocation cannot live in a community or commit to the vowed life due to their lifestyle. Despite this, some individuals may still be determined to pursue a consecrated celibate way of life because they believe it is their calling. When an individual who thinks that she is answering this call is dispelled from religious life, it can create a void and potentially lead to emotional trauma if they don't receive counseling. This situation can be particularly challenging in certain cultures, where a social stigma is attached to the individual and their family.

In some African cultures, religious vocation is highly esteemed, and religious members are revered;

some parents hope for their children to choose a consecrated celibate life. However, when a person leaves religious life, it can be a challenging experience for their family. Alternatively, in some cultures, dedicated religious life is looked down upon and seen as a "waste of resources" because young adults are expected to marry and have children to continue the family line. In this culture, the departure of this candidate from religious life is a cause for celebration.

Consecrated life is not unfamiliar to many African cultures. The continent of Africa historically practiced a specific form of consecrated life, in which a chosen individual was set apart for the gods, and some of them remained unmarried. It was the missionary activities in the continent that gave rise to institutionalized religious groups (Kiaziku, 2007, pp. 31-32). The sense of solidarity and community living is essential to African cultural values, and children are considered a gift to their parents and the entire society, including the Church. Therefore, when a young adult decides to join religious life, it brings joy to the family and the community, particularly in some African cultures where consecrated life is highly valued (Ogbuji, 2019). This holy sacrifice of joining religious life is regarded as noble and a welcome gesture. Kiaziku explains further that a person who consecrates their life to God and for the sake of the people has much relevance and is presented as a qualified mediator between God and humanity (p. 32). No wonder it is a cause for celebration, with solemn liturgy and family members and friends, when a religious person makes perpetual vows.

On the other hand, being dismissed from religious life is often considered a serious and socially unacceptable issue in many cultures. Out of the 110 religious people who participated in answering the question of whether social stigma affects ex-religious persons, a total of 81 participants confirmed to some degree that the dismissal has adverse effects on former members. The effects may be related to how the dismissal process was handled. The Canon Law states: When proper procedures of the Canon Law are applied during the dismissal of a member, it protects the rights of the dismissed rather than destroy them; it also upholds the name of the Church rather than disfigure the image of the Church (#1350).

The negative effects of leaving religious life can also be attributed to the adverse attitude that some cultures have toward those who leave religious life. This negative perception is not surprising given the sacredness and reverence with which the act of dedicating oneself to God is viewed in certain cultures. According to Zoundi (2016), the dismissal of a religious person in Africa appears to be a source of shame for the family, if not for the entire village (p. 123). No wonder some former members try to hold on to their religious attire or pretend to maintain their religious identity. They may be struggling with feelings of bitterness, anger, humiliation, shame, self-pity, self-blame, guilt, social stigma, and rejection from family and society. These experiences can sometimes lead to trauma-related disorders, depression, or a loss of faith. However, it is not a significant issue in our modern societies. Some parents would even be happy to have their children back.

Ex-religious # 26 explained, "Being dismissed from religious life was seen as a bad omen, associated with misfortune, and led to societal rejection. The pain I experienced led to deep depression. Similarly, the shame my family felt caused them great trauma and deeply affected their faith in the Catholic Church."

Ex-religious # 6 explained, "Religious persons are offered as gifts to God. And when they are dismissed, it is compared to the rejection of the sacrifice offered to God. That was how I felt."

The leaders of congregations, formators, and sisters without leadership or formation roles were asked whether social stigma affects former religious individuals. Below are some of their responses:

- Dismissed members of religious congregations often face rejection and isolation from society and family, and are sometimes treated as outcasts. This can have a profound impact on their well-being and sense of belonging.
- Some former members quickly adapt to their new situation, while others become bitter and distance themselves from family and friends. Some still wear religious attire as they live in shame and denial.
- Those who are deeply resentful are more affected, leading to depression and trauma-related issues. They may not be shunned by society, but they feel rejected and struggle to adjust to their new way of life.

- In my culture, departing from religious life is not viewed positively. People often believe that there is something wrong with the person who leaves. As a result, dismissed religious members from my culture may struggle to cope with life and end up feeling sorry for themselves.
- Yes, to some extent, individuals who have left religious life may experience suicidal thoughts. I know someone who nearly took her own life because her family rejected her. However, those who left voluntarily are content.
- I feel like there is a mystery behind leaving religious life. Sometimes, I wonder why misfortunes seem to follow those who have left the religious life. Those who are divorced can cope with life; why can't some dismiss religious people? A few years ago, a dismissed religious killed herself because she was not allowed to make perpetual vows. This issue is a severe social and religious concern.
- A social stigma exists in my culture because it is seen as a shame & disgrace to the families.

- The person and her family are mostly affected and might harbor bitterness for the congregation, especially when the dismissal process was not in accordance with Canon Law.
- In the past, society had trouble accepting dismissed members, but today it is no longer an issue.
- Dismissed individuals and their families often face challenging experiences, particularly in rural areas. This is less common in urban areas, which is why many individuals who have been dismissed from religious life avoid visiting their community.
- I have observed that some former members who were dismissed developed mental health issues due to feelings of depression and anger.
- Those who left on their own are happy, but those dismissed unjustly are bitter. And social stigma does not exist in these modern times.
- Society sometimes rejects them. They endure loneliness, their families face ridicule, and people view them as failures, especially when they struggle to manage their lives effectively.

Smith (2017) writes: "I've seen it too often. A young Catholic man or woman leaves the seminary or novitiate and then leaves the Church altogether because the pain and confusion they experience are so great; some express a sense of sadness and loss, a feeling that God is no longer present to them, for years, sometimes decades, afterward." This confirms what Nakato (2016) noted: some former religious members find dismissal humiliating and demoralizing because people may start imagining the possible offense of the person, relatives of the dismissed take it as a rejection of the family, and may stop attending church. Some dismissed religious also suffer rejection from their family members because such dismissal is taken as a curse on the family (pp. 114-115). Just as families, friends, and relatives celebrate and ritualize with joy the profession of vows of their relative who joined the congregation, they mourn with dismay the departure of a relative or friend from the convent.

The Process of Separation from Consecrated Life

Discontinuation of a member from consecrated life is a juridic act. A juridic act is a human action recognized by law as having legal effects (Nakato, p. 118). Nakato continues that when the leaders neglect the formalities of the juridic act or legal process for dismissal, the dismissal becomes invalid. This includes not providing written and signed warnings, allowing the accused to defend themselves, conducting a proper investigation to gather adequate information before dismissing a member, and issuing a written letter of dismissal (p. 119, Can. 127). In fact, the Canon Law warns that those who cause harm to others by malicious juridic acts are obliged to repair the damages done (Can. 128).

Dismissal of religious persons is the canonical procedure of terminating a member's incorporation in the institute (Nakato, p. 113). During this process, formators and leaders need to have access to appropriate information and allow members the opportunity to defend themselves before the dismissal process can be considered fair and just. The individual has the right to human dignity (Can. 208), respect for the right to fair judgment and according to the law (Can 221), respect for the right of defense (Can. 221), and respect for the circumstances that can affect the imputability (Can. 1323-1325; Lezohupski, 2016, p.108-109).

According to the Canon Law (684-704), a formee or a full member of a congregation (religious in perpetual vows) can be separated from the order in three ways:

- Transfer to another religious congregation: Through the permission and consent of the superiors and the councils of the giving and receiving congregations, a member of one order can transfer to another after three years of probation, but not novitiate in the new institute (Lezohupski, 107, Can. 684-685).
- Departure from the institute: This can be distinguished between exclaustration and expulsion. Exclaustration is the temporary departure or permission to temporarily live outside the convent given by the superior for up to 3 years. It can happen using an indult (conces-

> sion) or imposed for a grave reason. Expulsion or definitive departure takes place at the expiration of the temporary profession when the individual decides to abandon the institute without renewing one's vow for just and grave reasons (Can. 688) or by an indult to leave the institute definitively requested by the perpetually professed member (Can. 690) and approved by the Holy See if the institute is of pontifical right or by the local bishop if it is of a diocesan right (Lezohupski, 107-108).

Dismissal of members can be automatic for grave reasons such as defecting from the Catholic faith, contracting or attempting to contract marriage, stubborn disobedience to the legitimate prescripts of superiors in a grave matter, grave scandal arising from the culpable behavior of the member, stubborn upholding of doctrines condemned by the magisterium of the Church, public adherence to ideologies infected by materialism or atheism, etc (Can. 694-696). This is known as *Ipso Facto* (Automatic Dismissal). The proof must be gathered and presented to the council for automatic dismissal. Another type of dismissal is *Ab Homine* or mandatory dismissal (Lezohupski, p. 108). On this, Can. 695 stated that "the superior can decide that dismissal is not completely necessary and that correction of the member, restitution of justice, and reparation of scandal can be resolved sufficiently in another way." Can. 696 §2 states that even causes of lesser gravity established in proper law are sufficient for the dismissal of a member in temporary vows.

Alternatively, a member may be dismissed from the congregation if she is found to be incapable of living the charism and the way of life of the congregation, as outlined in the institute's constitutions (Lezohupski, p.109). Other impediments to separation may include certain physical, mental, or emotional disabilities (Collins 2017). This is true because individuals who desire a religious life must be physically and emotionally capable and stable in order to fulfill all the requirements of their vocation.

Nevertheless, Can 1321 explains that no one is punished through dismissal unless the external violation of a law or precept committed by the person is gravely imputable by reason of malice or negligence

(Can. 1321 §1). Inasmuch as dismissal is used as a means of punishment when a member commits a grave sin, however, it should be used as a last resort when other lighter disciplines such as warnings, fraternal corrections, and exclaustration have been applied (Can. 1341, 1348, 1733). Nakato (2016) noted that while many religious institutes follow the correct procedure in their dismissal process, many also have used awkward scenarios that portray the spirit of lawlessness exhibited during the dismissal of members, which has not only affected the dismissed religious but also the institutes and the church at large (P. 114).

One of the questions asked the participants during the data collection was whether the separation process followed the appropriate procedure. The researcher noted that there was much hesitation among the leaders and the formators to answer this question. 63% of the leaders strongly agree that they follow the appropriate process, but 37% express that the process sometimes does not follow the proper procedure. This is because some leaders have dismissed members when they felt threatened and uncomfortable with them. Sometimes, there is bias, incorrect information, hatred, tribal sentiment, prejudice, etc. 73% of the formators agreed that they follow the proper process, while 27% disagreed, stating that sometimes hasty decisions were made and innocent members were sent home. From the control group, 25% of the participants agree that the separation process follows the proper method, whereas 70% of the population disagree that the process sometimes follows a cruel procedure. The control group explained that sometimes leaders may have half-truths and conspire against those who challenge them, resulting in the person being sent away. Other times, the process is influenced by tribalism, personality clashes, jealousy, lies, and gossip. Additionally, 5% of the control group were unsure about how the process is carried out.

The findings of this research confirm that many congregations adhere to Canon Law and their constitution when dismissing a member, indicating that they follow the proper process. However, there is also evidence that, at times, leaders and formators may be biased and influenced by gossip, unfounded rumors, prejudice, and tribal sentiments. Thus, the dismissal process is often completed without gathering enough information. Some individuals have been dismissed orally without an official letter, as suggested by Canon Law, such as in the cases of ex-religious members 22 and 26. Others, such as ex-religious member 23, were dismissed via Skype. Smith (2017) enlightens, "The manner in which some members are separated from the convent can be disturbing. Too often, when a young man or woman decides to leave the seminary or religious life, little or no attention is given to what will happen to them emotionally and spiritually afterward. It is as if the person leaving is no longer their concern."

A leader who participated in this research explained: "Sometimes, members are sent away due to misunderstandings. I know of a sister who was sent away because of an unfounded accusation. After a few months, the truth was revealed, but her reputation had already been damaged. When asked to return to the congregation, she was so bitter and angry to return." Another participant in the leadership position explained: "At times, we witness injustice, biased leadership, and prejudice, which can lead to division among council members."

This confirms what Nakato (2016) stated: sometimes the spirit of lawlessness is demonstrated in dismissals, affecting the dismissed individuals, the religious institute, and the church as a whole. Interviewees 20, 18, 11, and 8, who were falsely accused and sent away, confirmed this. Clearly, it is appropriate to gather sufficient information from both parties, carefully discern, and pray earnestly before dismissing a member to minimize the pain inflicted on former members of the religious community.

Another question posed to the leaders and formators involved in this study was: **"Do you have sufficient information prior to separating a member?"** Nineteen leaders affirmed they had sufficient information, while eleven leaders dissented. Twenty-two formators strongly agree that they have adequate information, while eight formators admit that sometimes they don't. Some of the leaders' responses are below:

- Yes, the necessary information is gathered, and the individual is given multiple warnings. However, sometimes decisions are made hastily due to gossip and nepotism, which is really unfortunate. I feel upset when former members aren't given a chance to defend themselves. It's essential to adhere to Canon Law and ensure that everyone's right to self-defense is respected.

- At times, the process is done properly, and we have enough information. At other times, we are carried away by prejudice, wickedness, and hatred, and fail to follow our constitution. Sometimes, the leadership team is divided, and it is the former members who ultimately suffer. My heart goes out to them!
- Sometimes, there is infighting among leaders and an unforgiving spirit. Some members are falsely accused and sent home. When the truth is discovered, we leaders are ashamed and divided in asking the ex-member to return to the congregation.

Some responses from the formators:

- Yes, accurate information is gathered before the separation process is completed. We follow our constitutions and give several verbal and written warnings. However, if the person is not improving, she is asked to leave. Often, parents are involved, engaging in dialogue with the individual as she navigates her personal growth. Counseling may be sought, and dismissal can occur if the desired lifestyle is not maintained.

- Sometimes, a formation process may be discontinued due to personality clashes or differences, especially if a formator feels threatened by a strong character or a more knowledgeable formee. We are human, and sometimes we make mistakes and recommend the dismissal of an innocent formee simply because of a personality clash.
- Yes, an appropriate process is followed. The person is given several warnings, and we also involve the parents. Sometimes, the leaders dismiss a member even after the formator recommends the person for perpetual vows. At that time, we, as formators, had no power to stop their decision. Sometimes, we rely on information provided by community mem-

bers and dismiss a candidate without verifying the information or hearing from the person.

- Sometimes, yes; and other times, prejudice and personality differences can interfere with the fair treatment of members in initial formation. In some cases, certain members are favored and protected by those in authority, regardless of their wrongdoings, while others are treated with disdain, and even a minor mistake can cost them their religious vocation. Sometimes, jealousy among formation team members creates division; ultimately, the person who suffers is the formee.

The control group (consisting of sisters who are neither leaders nor formators) was asked the same question: **"Do your leaders/formators have enough information before the separation of a sister?"** Fourteen Sisters strongly agreed, nine sisters were unsure, and twenty-seven believed the leaders and formators sometimes do not have enough information before a sister is separated from the congregation. Below are some of their responses:

- Yes, the leaders have enough information, and we follow the Canon Law and our constitution. The process is thorough and adequate. It takes time, especially for perpetually professed sisters, because dispensation from Rome takes longer. Warning letters are usually given to the person, and we follow the directives of our congregation. Other times, the process is hurriedly completed without sufficient information. Sometimes, the outcome depends on the individual's case, leading to the use of different measures and favoritism.
- Yes and no: sometimes, the information is one-sided, and prejudice can creep in. Ex-members are sometimes not allowed to defend themselves. The dismissal process in my congregation is sometimes ruthless. I wonder whether our leaders engage in the discernment process by invoking the guidance of the Holy Spirit. Occasionally, our leaders and formators are very uncharitable.
- The process is unfair sometimes because a formee might be dismissed for flimsy reasons, such as asking a challenging question to

a formator or having a healthy relationship with a priest. The formation house becomes a "purgatory" where the formee is not allowed to speak freely for fear of being sent away. We form people who seem to be fearful, and their true selves become apparent when they make perpetual vows.

- Sometimes formators have favorite formees who are treated better than the rest, while others are closely watched for any mistake. As a result, many formees feel compelled to wear masks to please their formator. There is a lack of charity and fairness sometimes in the formation house, especially when a formee is not in the "good books" of the formator.
- Sometimes, there is a lack of proper discernment because leaders rely on the evaluation of community members or the formation team without hearing from the person directly. Therefore, when an individual is relocated to a new community due to a challenging situation in their previous community, the news of the situation reaches the new

community before the person arrives. As a result, the person is judged and condemned based on the communicated information rather than who they really are.

- Our leaders are not always transparent, and the victims often feel bitter after a haphazard process. Sometimes, our leaders tell only half-truths and may conspire against those who challenge them. Tribalism, personality differences, jealousy, lies, and gossip can affect their decision-making process.

When the same question was posed to the dismissed religious members about whether the process of their separation from the consecrated life followed the appropriate procedure, here are some of their responses.

Ex-religious # 1: The process was unjust because I was not given a chance to explain myself or be heard. This sentiment was echoed by fourteen other participants.

Ex-religious # 8: I received multiple warnings, and the proper protocol was followed before I was asked to leave. I was fully prepared for this. This was also reiterated by an additional sixteen participants.

Ex-religious # 17: The process was unfair because I wasn't given a chance to improve. Instead of constructive feedback, my supervisor resorted to verbal attacks and name-calling. I understand that nobody is perfect, but everyone deserves to be treated with respect.

Ex-religious # 18: No, the process was filled with baseless rumors, gossip, conspiracy, and tribal sentiment. This was reaffirmed by twelve other participants.

Based on the collected data from participants in groups 1, 2, 3, and 4, it is evident that a significant number of leaders, formators, as well as a few religious and ex-sisters firmly believe that the dismissal process follows the correct canonical procedure. Several warnings are given to the departing member; the constitutions and Canon Law are adhered to.

On the other hand, some leaders, formators, as well as most of the participants in the control group (consecrated individuals who are not in leadership or training roles), and the majority of the dismissed religious, believed that personality differences, animosity, disagreements, baseless rumors, prejudice, bias, favoritism, gossip, tribalism, misunderstandings, and divided leadership teams, impact the decision-making process of leaders in reaching a fair judgment for members who are leaving the congregation Nakato (2016) explained that often, former members were not told what they had done, were not shown compassion, and were not given the opportunity for a fair hearing. Some were treated with contempt, and verbal attacks were sometimes used. Nakato explicates further that some congregation leaders are carried away by unlimited power, which they sometimes misuse by dismissing members without proper procedures, council consent, or written warnings. (Nakato, 2016, p. 114-116).

The Canon Law is clear about the dismissal process, stating that members should be warned verbally and in writing, and that they have the right to a fair hearing. When religious individuals receive separation letters without prior warnings or the chance to defend themselves, it is not charitable. This action damages the person's reputation and the church. (Can. 1350). Granted, there are times when the offense is so serious that the leaders can use *Ipso Facto* (Automatic Dismissal). However, it is always important to hear the member's side of the story when they are asked to leave.

The process of discontinuing a member can be very challenging and should be done with kindness, care, sensitivity, and caution. A lack of kindness and charity can damage the relationship between the dismissed member and the congregation. Nakato emphasizes that this lack of charity is evident in the unfriendly remarks exchanged between dismissed members and leaders, as well as in the lack of support shown by some institutes toward dismissed members. This includes denying them financial and psychological assistance to help them adjust to life in the secular world (p. 116). It is inappropriate for leaders and individuals to be separated from the congregation to engage in contentious comments or unfriendly arguments, as this can cause emotional distress for the dismissed members.

The process of leaving religious life is smoother when members discern and realize that they are called to a different kind of vocation and request to leave. When an individual is struggling with religious life, for example, feeling unhappy or unfulfilled, they can ask for exclaustration or request to leave the congregation. Zoundi (2016) concurs that when an individual voluntarily leaves religious life, they depart the institute feeling content and at peace (p.121). This results in a smooth discontinuation, and the former member maintains a positive relationship with the institute.

Below are some responses from former religious individuals who reported experiencing freedom and happiness after leaving their religious life.

Ex-religious 19: I left religious life of my own accord. Coping with life after that wasn't easy, but I am happy with my decision. I still visit the sisters because they are my friends.

Ex-religious individuals 46, 45, and 48 left religious life because they wanted to start their own families and have children. They expressed that leaving brought them joy and peace because they were never meant for a religious vocation. They are now happily married and still maintain a relationship with their former religious institutes.

On the other hand, some members prefer to stay in the institute even after realizing that they are not called to consecrated life or after committing a grave sin. This can cause significant tension within the community, especially when the leaders and council members are at odds. (Zoundi, p.121). Nakato agreed that a lack of unity among leaders could lead to the general superior dismissing a member without the council's approval, invalidating the act itself (p. 115). This can cause chaos in religious institutes and may confuse those who are dismissed. It's essential to handle the process compassionately, even though it can be challenging for some members to understand that they are not called to a particular congregation.

Ex-religious # 17 had a similar experience. She said, "My formator never provided feedback on areas for improvement, but one day I received a dismissal letter in an unkind manner. I was unprepared for this, and it led to several months of emotional breakdown and confusion. I experienced panic attacks and constant anxiety. I turned to overeating and gained weight due to depression, feeling that my life was meaningless. My family was also upset and decided to switch to a different Christian denomination."

Finally, some members are terminated due to leaders' malice and tribal sentiments, not because of any grave offense committed by the person (Nakato, p.116). Of course, Canon Law disapproves of this behavior (Can. 128) and warns against malicious legal actions. This was discovered to be the fate of some former religious individuals during the research:

Ex-religious # 18: I was unfairly dismissed due to jealousy, unfounded rumors, gossip, and conspiracy theories without proper consideration. The impact was extremely painful and traumatic. I felt like a failure, confused, ashamed, and rejected. It felt like the purpose and meaning in my life were taken away, especially when my family members rejected me. I even considered suicide, but with the help of therapy, I was able to overcome those thoughts. Recently, the council members who judged me without hearing my side of the story apologized for relying on gossip and rumors. I was glad they found out the truth, but the damage it caused me ran deep.

Ex-religious # 23: I was separated from the congregation via Skype because I was accused of not showing respect to the leaders. I did not receive any official notification. I am now married with two children, but I still harbor deep bitterness over the way I was treated. I suffered from depression for many years, and my family felt betrayed and faced social rejection. I no longer attend church due to the trauma.

Ex-religious # 26: I was verbally dismissed from the congregation without any warning or a formal letter from the leaders. I was told that I didn't share their spirituality and that I was too vocal and rude. This experience led to suffering from insomnia and social stigma as the leaders favored the opinion of the formator over mine, eventually leading to rejection from my family.

Zoundi tells a story of how a young, professed sister was sent away from her congregation by her leader without any respect for due process. She was sent away because she attempted to help her congregation clarify some unclear rules in one of their documents. Zoundi warned this leader against her action, but he was told that it was the leader's issue and that she didn't need anyone's advice. After some months, the diocese's bishop replaced this leader with a new one, and the sister was called back (p. 123).

Ex-religious # 20 had the same experience of leaving the convent maliciously. She explained, "The leaders hastily decided that I should leave the convent, which was devastating. I had to carry the weight of a sin I never committed. When the truth was finally revealed, I had already endured so much humiliation. The trauma was so intense that I struggled to function in society. I had to go into hiding because nobody believed in my innocence, and my family disowned me for bringing shame upon them. Although I was eventually vindicated and called back to the Congregation, the damage had already been done, and I never returned."

Dismissal can be peaceful if the leaders and formation personnel approach the decision with fairness and accompany the person with compassion, respecting their dignity, and avoiding a cold and callous attitude during the discontinuation process. When leaders dismiss members without following proper procedures, without the consent of the council members, and without written and signed warnings, it can lead to trauma-related problems, depression, anxiety-related issues, and an inability to cope in the secular world.

The results from this work confirmed the fear of the Catholic bishops of Kenya (2014): "We express fear about the state of ex-religious who have left their institutes.... Some find dismissal humiliating and demoralizing because people assume all possible offenses they have committed in order to be expelled. Some parents and relatives of the dismissed felt a sense of weakness in their faith and interpreted it as the church's rejection of the whole family. Some dismissed members are also rejected by their families because such dismissals are taken as a curse on the family. At the same time, some remain as outcasts if they do not find understanding with their former religious institutes" (p. 6).

Former members who leave religious life on their own accord are unaffected by social stigma, and they are happy, while those who feel mistreated tend to blame themselves and feel sorry for themselves. Can these individuals learn coping skills, stop blaming religious leaders, and challenge negative self-pitying thoughts? Quoting cognitive therapy, Corey (2015) clarifies that blame lies at the core of emotional disturbances (p. 293). When an ex-religious person stops blaming themselves and others, learn to take responsibility, and finds meaning in a painful situation, they will not be affected by societal rejection. The questions to ponder are: Why is there so much anger and trauma in some former religious individuals? What procedures can be applied during the dismissal process to be more compassionate and humane in order to minimize hurt?

Chapter Four

Trauma of Separating from Consecrated Life

Trauma is a global issue with significant and far-reaching impacts on individuals and society. Internationally, trauma is ranked as the sixth leading cause of death and the fifth leading cause of moderate and severe disability (Taher, Shuja, and Amir, 2015, p. 1). In 2025, the World Health Organization (WHO) reports that major trauma is the eighth leading cause of death across all age groups and the leading cause of death among children and young adults (Halvachizadeh, S., et al. 2025). Trauma is real! Emotional pain is real! It kills and can have devastating consequences. It inflicts deep pain, wounds, and fear in victims, profoundly affecting their lives. We must acknowledge its impact and take it seriously.

Psychological trauma is an experience that is emotionally painful, distressful, or shocking, which often results in lasting mental and physical effects. (Schnurr and Green, 2004). Trauma can result from exposure to violence, abuse, divorce, vehicle accidents, severe injury, threatened death, natural disasters, wars, terrorist attacks, severe stressful experiences, etc. These experiences can impact a person's cognitive, behavioral, physical, spiritual, and psychological well-being, potentially leading to the development of Acute Stress Disorder (ASD), posttraumatic stress disorder (PTSD), panic disorder, or major depressive disorder.

The person diagnosed with ASD may have the following response: intense fear, helplessness, or horror. For PTSD, the person may experience flashbacks, fear, severe anxiety, mistrust, insomnia or nightmares, social isolation, etc. Panic Disorder may cause rapid heartbeat, feelings of fear or terror, dizziness, and difficulty breathing (Jeenah and Moosa, 2017, p. 586). Depression is characterized by feelings of hopelessness, despair, lack of interest in previously enjoyed activities, and difficulty concentrating (DSM-5-TR, 2022; Jeenah and Moosa, 2017, p. 586).

Symptoms of Trauma according to Despres (2017)

1. Shock, Denial, or Disbelief: After psychological trauma, individuals may seem shaken, disoriented, and disconnected. This signifies a coping mechanism and a need for assistance.
2. Aggression: Trauma can lead to aggression, either directed inward as self-blame and shame or outward as bursts of aggressive behavior, mood swings, and irritability.
3. Issues with sleeping: Experiencing a traumatic event can lead to sleep disruptions such as difficulty falling or staying asleep, nightmares, flashbacks, or night terrors related to the event.
4. Anxiety: Experiencing trauma often leads to anxiety, triggered by thoughts or visual images of the event, resulting in overwhelming fear and panic attacks.
5. Disassociation: This is the process of detaching emotions from events when trauma structurally and functionally alters the brain,

leading to memory loss and withdrawal from others.

6. Physical symptoms: Trauma can cause physical problems like body pain, stomach issues, and muscle tension. It can also lead to feelings of edginess, and one is easily agitated.

Trauma is a significant issue for some individuals who have left religious life. Life after leaving the convent can be challenging, with some former sisters experiencing freedom and others experiencing trauma-related symptoms. Daly (2020) expressed that "Studies show that women's experiences of this transition vary widely. Some don't have trouble with it at all. Some, however, experience it as a downright trauma and, depending on various factors, may respond with such drastic behaviors as descending into addiction and risky activity, leaving the Church, or even contemplating suicide.[5]

One of the respondents to Daly's post said, "Thank you for your article. I have never recovered

[5] https://www.hprweb.com/2020/ 01/pastoral-care-of-women-who-have-left-the-convent/

from the trauma of being sent out of the convent after ten years of being in it. Even after being appointed as the novice director for three years and after the founder passed away, I was told to leave due to an "obedience" issue. Well, it was due to politics for sure."

Another respondent explained: "I can relate to her. It took me ten years after leaving the convent to realize that I was in trouble spiritually and emotionally. I have been in therapy for almost four years, and I couldn't have made it this far without my therapist."

Christina M. Sorrentino (2023), a blogger and theology teacher in New York, also expressed: "I can personally attest to the loneliness and overwhelming grief that can follow leaving the convent. When I left the convent for the second time several years ago, I felt lost and broken. The pain I experienced was all-consuming, and I feared I would never recover. It wasn't until I connected with other women who had similar experiences through online support groups that I began to heal." She continues: "Many women who have left the convent experience grief, heartache, depression, anxiety, post-traumatic stress disorder, anger, resentment, and a range of other emotions resulting from possible traumatic experiences within the convent walls."[6]

Until trauma-related behavior was identified among some former religious individuals, the departure of individuals from the convent may not have been a cause for concern. The trauma associated with leaving religious life has now become a societal issue. The Kenya Conference of Catholic Bishops (2014) noted this concern: "We noted with fear the state of ex-religious who have left their institutes and continue to retain and parade in the habits of their former institutes pretending to still belong to the order, others form associations which they take as equivalent to religious institutes, while others go to the extent of soliciting funds in the name of their former institutes and even recruit new members to these associations (p. 6). Why do some former members of religious orders continue to wear the habit or religious attire of their previous order in the pretense of

---

[6] https://catholicexchange.com/helping-former-nuns-transition-back-into-the-world/

being religious individuals? Why are some ex-religious individuals confused and bitter, wallowing in self-pity and misery, while others have successfully adjusted to society and found happiness?

During data collection, a significant number of participants confirmed that individuals who have left their religious communities experience emotional trauma. Specifically, 76.7% of the leaders, 56.6% of formators, and 78.9% of active members agreed that many former religious individuals and their family members suffer from trauma-related symptoms. Apart from those who freely left religious life, 90% of those who were dismissed described the process as traumatic. Some former religious individuals reported experiencing the trauma-related symptoms mentioned below. Here are a few of their responses:

Ex-religious # 2: I was a perpetually professed sister when I was thrown out of the congregation. I found myself in disagreement with the authority. Despite my efforts to explain my side of the story, none of the counselors supported me and instead sided with the superior general. This led to a dismissal process, and I was abruptly terminated without receiving formal written notice. I felt betrayed, angry, confused, and traumatized by the experience. For two years, I struggled to cope and adjust to society. I wore a habit that I made for myself and lived pretending to be someone I wasn't. I eventually left the Catholic faith, but life didn't improve. My family members were disheartened after facing ridicule from the community, and they lost faith in Catholicism as well. I wish I had received counseling at the time, but I couldn't afford it. The congregation didn't provide financial assistance. Even though I have a job now, I still feel angry and traumatized when I encounter reminders of religious life.

Ex-religious # 3: I struggled with self-esteem and needed to reclaim the ability to think for myself rather than being told what to do every day. I wanted to take responsibility for my life and be free. The decision to leave religious life brought joy to my life, although initially, I struggled with it and was reluctant to leave. When I finally decided to leave the convent, I felt a sense of relief and joy.

Ex-religious # 4: The trauma I experienced due to the sexual abuse by my formator led me to leave religious life. I harbored deep resentment toward the church and everything it stood for, feeling used, wounded, and vulnerable.

Ex-religious # 6: After spending many years in religious life, I decided to leave due to a challenging and difficult period of formation. Life after leaving the religious community was complicated. I felt lonely and isolated as all my friends had deserted me. However, after finding a job, I became happy and content. Initially, my family was ashamed due to the name-calling, but they have become more accepting over time.

Ex-religious # 13: I left on my own accord because some religious personnel, especially our leaders, were becoming hypocritical. I was furious because the congregation didn't support me. My decision initially disappointed my family, but they eventually came around and supported me. I feel good serving God as a layperson rather than living a pharisaic life.

Ex-religious # 11: I requested to renew my vows, but it was not approved. I was then asked to leave religious life without being given any information about what I did wrong. This news had a chaotic effect on me. I developed severe depressive symptoms, including insomnia, persistent sadness, feelings of hopelessness, guilt, pessimism, worthlessness, and helplessness. I also lost interest in my favorite hobby, and my family members were affected by the situation.

Ex-religious # 10: The impact of leaving religious life was devastating and intolerable. Despite the financial support from the sisters, I yearned to understand my mistakes.

Ex-religious # 9: The impact was distressing, harrowing, and humiliating. I couldn't go back home for many years because I felt so ashamed. My superior didn't approve my request to renew my vow, so it expired. I felt wounded and hurt. The accusation against me was later found to be false, but at that point, it was too overwhelming to return to religious life, and I was already in a committed relationship.

Ex-religious # 12: I tallied with another sister as a chapter delegate. However, when she was chosen over me due to her age (I was younger), the leaders made life difficult for me. I was unfairly judged and condemned for false issues without a trial, and eventually, I was dismissed. This experience caused me to suffer from depression and insomnia for many months. As a result, my family lost faith in the church and in the Congregation.

Ex-religious # 21: My request to make perpetual vows was denied without any preparation or warning. It felt like something had died inside me. I harbored so much anger and hatred toward the leaders and God that I stopped going to Mass. I cried daily, suffered from sleepless nights, and the burden of unforgiveness weighed me down. When I was leaving home for religious life, I was offering myself as a gift to God, but my dismissal from religious life felt like a rejection of this sacrifice.

Ex-religious # 25: I was told I prayed too much and was called to a more contemplative life. I was dismissed, and it was a painful experience. I suffered from depression and struggled to adapt to the secular world after leaving. I still wear the veil and am searching for a new congregation.

Ex-religious # 47: I struggled with bitterness, confusion, and depression for years, but with the support of my family, I found solace through faith in God. (This was also voiced by ex-religious numbers 49 and 50).

Ex-religious # 22: On that fateful day when I was handed a letter of dismissal, I felt demoralized and sobbed daily. I asked God so many questions and even tried to end my life because I couldn't bear the shame of false accusations. Thankfully, a friend rescued me. The pain was unbearable, and I suffered from ulcers and stomach problems. I wore a veil for a year before finally accepting the reality that I am no longer religious. My family members were deeply affected and wounded. They thought I had disgraced them and called me names. This was very painful and hard to bear.

Ex-religious # 28: I suffered from depression for months, experiencing sleepless nights, but with the support of my family and friends, I was able to find healing.

Ex-religious # 30: I was deeply traumatized and wounded, leading to the development of ulcers and sleepless nights. My faith in God was also affected.

Ex-religious # 42: I stepped down from my leadership role after being accused of misleading the congregation. It was a difficult and traumatic experience, but with the support of my family and psychotherapy, I have found happiness in serving God as a lay faithful.

Based on the results above, most individuals who leave religious life experience emotional trauma, severe depression, bitterness, anger, confusion, and to some extent, difficulty in adjusting to life outside the walls of the convent. The symptoms of trauma that Despres R. (2017) mentioned above were very much present. These included denial, shock, and disbelief, which were depicted in the wearing of the veil and the religious habit of former institutes. Some of the participants experienced insomnia, anxiety, aggression, shame, guilt, self-blame, anger, and physical symptoms such as ulcers. This is also in line with Winell's concept of Religious Trauma Syndrome, which she compares to the trauma of going through a divorce (2007, p.15).

On the other hand, those who voluntarily left consecrated life did not experience trauma, as indicated by some of their responses below:

Ex-religious # 27: I requested a one-year exclaustration, which was granted after our leaders conspired against me. I left following the end of the exclaustration period because I realized that religious life was not for me. I am now happily married (**Ex-religious #34 and 36 echoed the same sentiment**).

Ex-religious # 38, 39, 40, 41, 44, and 42 left after making their perpetual vows, and they are now happily serving God as lay faithful.

Indeed, trauma often brings an overwhelming amount of stress that can surpass one's ability to cope with or process the painful emotions involved. Religious trauma is a part of this overwhelming struggle, and it can lead to serious long-term negative consequences, as this work discovered.

Religious Trauma

Religion is often perceived as a source of comfort, meaning, and purpose for those experiencing challenging and adverse life events. Others perceive religion as a construct that may be closely associated with trauma adaptation. Some have proposed that religion integrates the seemingly incomprehensible trauma into a "sacred order"—providing the knowledge that even the traumatizing events have a place within the order of a larger universe (Berger, 1990). Many people have speculated that exposure to trauma may lead to changes in an individual's religious faith, causing them to either abandon it or embrace it more strongly (Fontana and Rosenheck, 2004).

Religion is an organized system of belief comprising official doctrines that concern itself with sacred objectives (Wald and Calhoun-Brown, 2007, p.

25). It is a formal institution guided by creeds, rituals, and a set of doctrines, values, and morals that guide those who adhere to its teachings. Quoting Karen Armstrong (1996, xvi), Wald and Calhoun-Brown illustrated the essence of religion:

> "When they have contemplated the world, human beings have always experienced a transcendence and mystery at the heart of existence. They have felt that it is deeply connected with themselves and the natural world, but it also goes beyond. However, we choose to define it. It has been called God, Brahma, or Nirvana. This transcendence has been a constant presence in human life. We have all experienced something similar, whatever our theological opinions are, when we listen to a great piece of music or hear a beautiful poem, and feel touched within and lifted momentarily, beyond ourselves (p. 25)."

Religion prompts humans to ponder the transcendent and the divine beyond human understanding. Despite increasing secularization, religion continues to be a significant influence on our daily political activities and moral conduct. Almost everyone knows that arguing about religion with others is impolite and potentially dangerous, especially with friends (Wald and Calhoun-Brown, p. 1). Religion is often handled with care and sensitivity due to its ability to evoke strong emotions in people. Some individuals prefer to discuss their spirituality rather than institutionalized religion.

Spirituality and religion serve as distinct sources of meaning and values for individuals. Mohr (2006) defines spirituality as the search for meaning and belief in a higher power. Spirituality is essential to human existence, and it is present in everyone. It is present even when it is denied by the most convinced atheist or existentialist who struggles with the meaning and purpose of life, even as they perceive life as godless (Schermer 2003, p. 21). Spirituality is generally considered broader than any particular religion one might practice, as it encompasses cognitive and philosophical aspects of thought, as well as emotional and behavioral aspects.

In the late 19th century, philosophy and psychology grew disillusioned with spirituality as intellectual and scientific progress increasingly negated humanity's spiritual core and led to a growing suspicion of it. Schermer argues that spirituality has recently gained recognition as a legitimate aspect of mainstream psychology. (p. 21). Today, there is a growing interest in spirituality, including meditation practices, mindfulness exercises, and spiritual readings. This trend is leading to the incorporation of spirituality in holistic healing as an alternative therapy for stress management and daily living.

Spiritual problems are gaining attention in today's world. Although it is a topic not often discussed, its inclusion in the newest DSM-5-TR (APA, 2022) as a diagnostic category classified as a "Religious or Spiritual Problem" (Z65.8), represents a significant breakthrough. It is important to acknowledge the distress caused by losing or questioning of faith, transitioning to a new faith, or reevaluating spiritual values. (p. 834). Apparently, religious and spiritual problems have become areas of concern and can lead to trauma-related stress.

Religious Trauma Syndrome (RTS):

Empirical research has explored extensively the trauma that goes with losses of different kinds, such as loss of parents, home, job, partner, children, and siblings, as well as other types of traumatic experiences, e.g., divorce, natural disasters, warfare, ethnic cleansing, child abuse, rape, domestic violence, terrorist attack, gun violence, etc., that contain specific stressors like physical or psychological injuries. The loss of faith is seldom discussed. There are documented stories of the effects that loss of faith and religious trauma have on individuals (Shafranske, 1991). Often, the loss of faith or a faith community can cause social problems. Barra, Carlson, and Maize (1993) write: The feelings of anger and resentment, emptiness and despair, sadness and isolation, and even relief could be seen in individuals struggling with the loss of previously comforting religious tenets and community identification" (p. 292).

Some of these feelings are evident among the ex-religious individuals interviewed, as shown below. Some ex-religious individuals expressed relief after leaving on their own, while those asked to leave felt despair and anger.

Ex-religious # 7: While studying abroad, I was accused of living an immoral life by a superior. She wanted me to be deported, but I decided to leave religious life and continue my education on scholarship with the generous support of some friends. I received a dismissal letter without being given the opportunity to explain my side of the story. I felt discouraged, bitter, and betrayed. The false accusation caused me many sleepless nights. Until now, my family, especially my mother, has been unaware of what happened. I fear that it would deeply upset her if she found out that I am no longer in religious life.

Ex-religious # 5: I had a disagreement with my superior over the terms of my work. She was too hard on me and didn't listen to my concerns. She fought hard to have me dismissed, despite some council members not agreeing with her. However, she managed to gain their approval with her strong personality. When this happened, I felt humiliated and betrayed. I was in denial for many months and continued to wear a religious habit. Initially, I wanted to sue the congregation, but on second thought, I decided to let it go. Now, I am receiving help and coping with the reality that I am no longer a sister.

Ex-religious #16: Challenging the leaders and formators caused me a great deal of trouble. It seemed like the leaders were afraid of being challenged, and when I did challenge them, I was treated as an enemy. They went to great lengths to undermine me. I was frustrated and disappointed with how my situation was handled. Nobody listened to me, and I felt isolated. I was dismissed maliciously and out of jealousy, without any warning. This had a big impact on my mother, who suffered a heart attack. I experienced sleepless nights and depression, but now I am getting therapy.

Ex-religious #15: I experienced a crisis of faith and ultimately chose to leave religious life because I was not happy. I am finding freedom and peace regardless of what people around me might think of me and their potential judgment.

The above dilemma, as described by most participants in this study, is what Winell (2012) referred to as Religious Trauma Syndrome (RTS). The RTS is used to describe the depths of mental despair experienced by those who have left particular religious groups. It is the condition experienced by people who are struggling with departing from a dogmatic religion and coping with indoctrination. Marlene Winell is an American psychologist, educator, and writer. In her research work and book, published in 2007, entitled "Leaving the Fold: A Guide for Former Fundamentalists and Others Leaving their Religion," Winell explores the trauma of leaving the faith from the perspective of Christian fundamentalists.

According to Winell, RTS is a traumatic condition experienced by people who are struggling with leaving an authoritarian and dogmatic religion. They might be experiencing the collapse of a deeply meaningful faith and the process of distancing themselves from a controlling community and way of life. Even though leaving a religious institution can be highly traumatic and has impacted numerous individuals, this form of religious trauma has not been widely recognized.

Ezeani (2016) acknowledges that while there has been a lot of focus on promoting and recruiting vocations, there hasn't been enough written about supporting and preparing individuals for discontinuation during the formation process. In other words, there needs to be more discussion and reflection on how to compassionately accompany individuals who, after entering formation, begin to show signs that they may need to pursue paths other than religious life. Although discontinuation can be confusing, depressing, and traumatic, it is important to give it adequate attention.

Winell, though writing from a fundamentalist perspective, compares the symptoms of leaving the fold (church) with the feelings associated with ending a marriage, such as grief, anger, guilt, depression, lowered self-esteem, and social isolation (p. 1). And whereas support for divorced individuals is readily available, there is little or no assistance for those who leave religious communities.

Jennifer Muñoz (2015), in her doctoral dissertation through the Institute for Psychological Sciences (now Divine Mercy University), expressed that "the number of women who experience exiting the convent as a trauma is not negligible. The nature of this trauma is most akin to that of losing a spouse or getting a divorce. This makes sense because, after all, religious life is fundamentally an espousal to Christ. If a woman has begun to enter into this reality emotionally, you would expect the break from relating to Christ in this way to be correspondingly painful."

Quoting Muñoz, Smith (2017) concurred that "the pain of leaving religious life is by analogy the pain and loss a person feels in a divorce. Ex-nuns experience a deep sense of emptiness, pain, and loss when they leave religious life, and this is a problem almost no one has written about, even though the problem and the pain are very real."

Certainly, religious life manifests in the Church as a beautiful marriage brought about by God, and religious people offer their whole existence as a continuous worship of God in love (can. 573, #1). Consequently, the consecrated celibate person becomes a spouse of Christ. It's important to note that every baptized Christian is considered a spouse of Christ, who is the head of the Church. God's love for us is eternal and profound, regardless of our religious affiliation, and God wants us to have an intimate relationship with Him.

If religious individuals enter into a covenantal marriage with God and the church, the dissolution of this union by either the religious institute or personal decision will undoubtedly bring about the symptoms Winell and Muñoz described. In this case, there is a shift from a consecrated celibate life and a special relationship with Jesus, their Spouse, to a more secular life. Because of this apparent divorce with the congregation, the ex-nun's grieving process seems to follow a similar pattern to that of those going through a divorce, including stages of denial, anger, protesting, depression, acceptance, and restructuring. This similarity to the grieving pattern of divorce sheds light on why leaving religious life can be very traumatic. Some wounded former religious have been so affected by this trauma that they have turned away from the church, from a relationship with God, and even contemplated suicide.

Winell explains that those most at risk of developing Religious Trauma Syndrome include people who are raised in their religion, sheltered from the rest of the world, very sincerely and personally involved with their religion, and from a very controlling form of religion. The symptoms include cognitive, affective, functional, and social or cultural "dysfunctions." They suffer everything from confusion, anxiety, panic attacks, sleep and eating disorders, and substance abuse to difficulty with decision-making and critical thinking, lack of meaning, suicidal ideation, and rupture of family and social networks (p. 17). For Winell, part of the coping difficulty is the anxiety of having to go through the process alone since the community, family, and friends' support may not always be available for the individual. This was also echoed by Nakato (2016), who concurred that sometimes ex-religious are not supported by families and friends, which causes loneliness and rejection.

Support From Families

This question was posed to former religious individuals: **How much support did you receive from your family?**

Some of the former religious individuals interviewed claimed that their family members did not support them. For example, ex-religious #13 and #20. Ex-religious #20 explained that her family members disowned her for bringing shame to them, and ex-religious #26 also faced family rejection. Some leaders who took part in this project also confirmed that some families do not support their children, while others are glad to have them back. Below are some of their responses:

- There is significant tension when a member of a religious order is dismissed without sufficient explanation. Families are left feeling bitter because they are not provided with a reason for the dismissal. This lack of transparency leads to anger, causing some families to leave the Catholic Church and leading some former members to lose faith.

- Many former religious individuals experience emotional and psychological challenges, requiring support to navigate life. Their ordeal also impacts their families, subjecting them to ridicule and prompting some to depart from the Church. Failure of ex-religious to cope with life leads to mental challenges, although some who left religious life are also very happy with life.
- Some families are happy to welcome their daughters back, while others consider it a disgrace to their family. This bitterness affects the vocation in the community, as families in that parish may not allow their daughters to join the congregation in question. Witnessing a parent's trauma and subsequent death due to their child leaving religious life is demoralizing. The said daughter is also struggling with guilt and has developed mental health challenges.

Former religious individuals often face numerous challenges, including adjusting to a new lifestyle, forming new friendships, and rebuilding their lives.

To successfully rebuild one's life after leaving a religious institute, an individual must progress through five phases, according to Winell. (2007, p. 17-20). These stages are not distinct in a formal sense; instead, there is an overlap between them, and a person may be in more than one phase simultaneously.

The phases are:

1. **Separation:** Being part of a religious community can be fulfilling when things are going well. It can meet emotional, spiritual, and financial needs. However, if the experience turns negative, some may start to distance themselves and eventually choose to leave. Sometimes, people struggle for a while and then give up, while others stay in a situation by rationalizing it, even if they are unhappy. The separation process might be traumatic for some and relatively easy for others (p. 17).
2. **Confusion:** Leaving a religious institute can cause a state of confusion, especially when asked to leave abruptly. This is because the community defines one's entire reality. The confusion arises when one has to start over

with a new lifestyle, make new friends, make decisions without community support, and manage financial needs. At this time, some feel like naïve children, incapable of thinking, even as adults, while others feel liberated and relieved, as if released from prison (pp. 17-18). Ex-religious # 13 exclaimed: "It was difficult to decide to leave religious life, but when I finally did, I felt like a big weight was lifted from my shoulders. I was free at last!" Ex-religious # 19 has the same experience. Ezeani (2016) and Gitau (2016) also affirmed that some former members of religious institutes experience a sense of relief when they decide to leave religious life.

3. **Avoidance:** During this phase, individuals who have left religious life may stop attending Mass and avoid any events that remind them of their past religious life. The reason for this avoidance is to distance themselves from their previous connection with God, especially for those who feel rejected by God and mistreated by religious authority. Ex-religious # 3 said: "I stopped going to Church

for two years because I felt abandoned by God." According to Winell, the loss of a relationship with God can be devastating, as though one's parents have died, and if one has a personal relationship with Jesus Christ, then a relationship is broken and a lover lost (p. 19).

4. **Feeling:** This describes the intense mixed feelings of anger, guilt, and grief that may emerge after leaving a religious institute. These feelings were experienced by some dismissed religious that were interviewed. The feelings may arise from reflecting on the many years devoted to religious life. There may be frustration over what feels like wasted time, the dissipating of youthful energy, and comparing one's accomplishments to those of peers, among other concerns (p. 20).
5. **Rebuilding**: Winell demonstrated that individuals who leave a religious group can find healing by discovering their inner worth and seeking help through counseling (p. 20). Sometimes, a person's identity can become

> completely overshadowed by being a member of a religious institute. However, upon leaving, it may be necessary to reassert, understand, and reclaim oneself. The process of healing for former members of religious groups can occur when they are willing to confront and work through the pain and trauma of leaving religious institutions and allow their inner strength to surface. And unless one adjusts and replaces key relationships in one's life, one may feel abandoned and lonely. Ex-religious # 29 confirmed this: "I felt extremely lonely and sad because I don't have a support group, except for a few friends. My parents and siblings rejected me. I even attempted suicide, but thankfully, a friend intervened and saved me. I am currently undergoing counseling."

Apparently, some former religious individuals who participated in this research work underwent the five phases of Religious Trauma Syndrome (RTS) as defined by Winell. When they were no longer surrounded by the comfort of the religious institute, they initially felt confused and avoided anything that reminded them of religious life, including not going to church and feeling abandoned by God. After this comes intense emotions, including anger, guilt, rejection, shame, and rage, which lasted for months or even years for some of those interviewed. The final stage is the rebuilding of self, which begins when the individual initiates the healing process (pp.17-20). On the other hand, those who requested to leave and those who left voluntarily coped with life and have adapted well.

Furthermore, when individuals dismissed from religious communities receive social, financial, psychological, and emotional support, they tend to become empowered and recover more quickly from their trauma, anger, and depression. Social support within the spiritual community has been linked to reduced levels of depression (Dew, Daniel, Goldston, and Koenig, 2008). This was supported by the data gathered from the former religious individuals during the interview. Some claimed they received support, which helped them cope with life, while others did not.

Support From the Congregation

The question they were asked was: **How *were you supported by your congregation?***

Fifteen former religious members claimed that they were supported financially, but did not receive emotional or psychological support. Five ex-members explained that they were given little money for transport back home, with no spiritual, emotional, or psychological support. Thirteen of them explained that they were given a few clothes to change into from their religious habit and transportation fare to return to their families. Four former members were supported and educated. Seven former members explained that they received financial support to help them get started until they found employment. They were also provided with counseling. Five former members stated they received only a small amount of financial aid ($100.00) after dedicating their youthful years to the consecrated life. They wished they had received counseling sessions.

When the same question was posed to leaders, formators, and sisters—neither leaders nor formators—regarding the support received by former members from the Congregation, twenty leaders agreed to a certain degree that the discontinued religious are supported. Only ten of them disagree that the separated sisters are not adequately supported. Sixteen formators agree to a certain degree that ex-sisters are supported, while fourteen participants disagree that they were not adequately supported. In the control group, which consists of individuals who are neither leaders nor formators, twenty participants agree to some extent that ex-sisters are adequately supported. Meanwhile, twenty-seven participants disagree that ex-sisters are adequately supported, with three unsure.

The data gathered from former religious persons, leaders, formators, and sisters suggest that some individuals who discontinued their consecrated religious lives were primarily supported financially, while a few received academic and emotional support. However, the majority of the individuals did not receive any support, apart from the transportation fare to return home and a small amount of cash. The results also showed that those who received emotional support and counseling were able to function well and adjust to life outside of the convent.

For instance, Ex-religious # 10 expressed:

> "Despite feeling depressed when I was asked to leave religious life, the support I received was very helpful. I was empowered through many sessions of therapy. I still keep in touch with the sisters because they genuinely showed interest in my well-being. I am now a happy laywoman, but my heart goes out to those who are still in denial about leaving religious life. While it was initially painful, life must go on."

The majority of the former sisters/nuns could have benefited and been empowered if they had received emotional, psychological, and spiritual support upon leaving religious life. The experience of Ex-religious # 21 confirmed that:

> "I was sent to school, but I could hardly concentrate in class, and my grades suffered as a result. I suffer from insomnia and find it hard to relate to people, especially religious men and women. I was depressed for many years

> as I contemplated the process that led to my dismissal. I still ask myself every day: what offense did I commit? If I had received emotional support or counseling, I might have come to terms with the dismissal process."

In studying the trauma of leaving religious life, this work discovered with concern that little to no attention is given to the psychological and emotional needs of dismissed religious individuals. Some are sent to school or provided with minimal financial aid, neither of which helps them heal or function effectively in society. Canon Law #1350 states that the institute should show charity to the dismissed members by providing material, spiritual, and psychological well-being. The need for psychological help is vital, as expressed by the dismissed religious sisters below:

Ex-religious # 30: The trauma of leaving religious life led me to a man who impregnated me and then abandoned me. Now, I am feeling bitter and depressed. Although I need psychological help, I am unable to afford it.

Ex-religious # 37: I require therapy to empower me to let go of my religious habits and accept that I am no longer a nun. The dismissal process left me mentally wounded, leading to bitterness and depression.

Ex-religious # 47: I felt very bitter, ashamed, and confused. I hope to be able to come to terms with the hostile and unkind treatment I received before being dismissed from religious life. I want to seek counseling, but financial constraints are impacting this decision. This sentiment was also shared by 8 other former religious sisters.

Ex-religious # 3: The congregation was sponsoring my education, but they stopped as soon as I was dismissed. Now, I can barely feed myself. While I want to move on from the pain of dismissal, I am struggling to provide for my family. I would have greatly appreciated some counseling.

Ex-religious # 22, # 29, and #43: I lived in denial for a year, and within that time, I was planning how to kill myself. I believed I was no good and saw no positive aspects of life. But a friend helped me find a psychologist who is currently helping me. I am regaining my life again.

Ex-religious # 13: Leaving religious life was a personal decision. I struggled to make this decision at the beginning, and I would have appreciated a counselor's help, but I am happy now. This was also echoed by former religious members, numbers 19, 34, 36, 38, 39, 40, 41, 42, 45, 48, and 46.

The data collected from the four groups that participated in this study indicate that counseling or therapy is essential and will support the recovery of individuals who have left their religious communities. The wound inflicted on an individual as a result of departing from religious life affects the person's mental, physical, emotional, and spiritual well-being, as these are integral aspects of the person. (Young and Cashwell, 2011). Life is interconnected, and individuals who have been hurt by the trauma of leaving religious life require therapeutic healing to restore their mental well-being, enhance their coping skills, release negative self-defeating thoughts, acknowledge their inner strengths, have faith in their ability to thrive, and confront their despair with bravery.

The Importance of Therapy in Embracing a New Horizon

No one can wallow in pain and expect transformation. Change and healing can be experienced when one mourns what was and explores new possibilities. Embracing a new horizon means actively engaging with new possibilities that extend beyond the pain of leaving religious life. The individual steps into a new phase of life that may be daunting, but is worth pursuing. Accepting challenges that promote personal growth can lead to new opportunities and perspectives. Therapy plays a crucial role in this journey, as it helps individuals in self-discovery and to develop mature coping skills, embrace openness to new experiences, question negative beliefs, and facilitate emotional healing. The CBT model is very crucial in questioning and reframing negative thoughts.

Cognitive Behavioral Therapy (CBT):

Therapy is a process aimed at improving an individual's overall well-being and mental health. It aims to reduce challenging behaviors, beliefs, compulsions, thoughts, or emotions, while also enhancing relationships and social skills (Ogbuji, 2019). The therapeutic process involves verbal expression to gain insights into self, others, and the environment. Therapists are not in business to change clients, give quick advice, or solve their problems; instead, they facilitate healing through genuine dialogue with their clients, promoting change and growth (Corey, 2015, p. 6).

Cognitive behavioral therapy (CBT) is a therapeutic approach based on the principle that maladaptive moods and behaviors can be changed by replacing distorted or inappropriate ways of thinking with healthier and more realistic thought patterns (Ogbuji, 2019). The CBT model believes that our thoughts influence our behavior. Humans possess the potential for self-actualization, but they can also be influenced toward self-destruction through indoctrination and philosophical conditioning. People have a natural inclination toward self-preservation, happiness, forming loving connections with others, personal growth, and self-actualization. Despite this, people can also contribute to their own destruction through negative thoughts, repeating the same mistakes, intolerance, and self-blame. Therefore, CBT aims to help clients accept themselves as human beings who will continue to make mistakes while learning to live more at peace with themselves (Corey, p. 292).

Aaron Beck identifies the cognitive triad as forms of hostile, helpless, or critical thinking that are typical of individuals with depression. These thoughts are categorized into three distinct groups, according to Krapp (2004):

- Negative ideas about self (I am stupid)
- Negative view of the world (the world is partial)
- Negative view of the future. (The future is hopeless)

As these three components interact, they interfere with standard cognitive processing, leading to impairments in perception, memory, and problem-solving. This can cause a person to become obsessed with negative thoughts. Beck explained that spending time reflecting on negative thoughts would lead patients to treat these thoughts as valid.

At this juncture, Beck's Hopelessness Scale (Corey, 2015) can be useful for measuring feelings of hopelessness and self-defeating or negative thoughts experienced by former members of religious communities. These feelings can hinder their ability to adapt to life outside the convent as they become trapped in feelings of failure, self-blame, self-pity, and confusion. The test results will help the former religious persons understand the harm they are causing themselves and enable the therapist to work with them to identify negative self-schemas and develop the appropriate skills to overcome them. The theory of Beck and other proponents of Cognitive Behavioral Therapy (CBT) is fully explained in my book "Influence of Childhood Experiences on Faith Development," which was published in 2019. Some CBT techniques include questioning negative thoughts, cognitive restructuring, reframing self-defeating thoughts, practicing positive self-talk, assertiveness training, relaxation exercises, psychoeducation, managing emotional reasoning, etc (Ogbuji, 2019). For instance, when you feel like you are not good enough or like a failure, ask yourself: "Is there any evidence that I am not good enough?" "Is there evidence that I am a failure?" For individuals who have left a religious group, CBT can help them unlearn negative thoughts and reactions toward their former congregation and themselves. They can learn to challenge their self-blame, self-pity, and negative beliefs, essentially becoming their own therapists.

In addition to cognitive therapy, psychospiritual therapy can assist former nuns who have experienced spiritual, mental, and physical trauma. This type of therapy allows individuals to tap into their personal belief systems and use their faith in a higher power to explore areas of conflict in their lives (Young and Cashwell, 2011). This is because psychospiritual therapy involves an increased capacity for compassion toward others and oneself, allowing one to experience and accept their pain and suffering more fully, and to work toward self-acceptance and healing. Thus, with the techniques of CBT and psychospiritual therapeutic processes, the wounded ex-religious sisters can work toward their wholeness and be empowered to manage their stress and coping abilities.

Counseling can help improve the well-being of some of the dismissed religious individuals who continue to wear the habit of their former institute. This demonstrates that they are psychologically and emotionally wounded and may still be in denial. They could benefit from facing reality instead of remaining in denial. Therapy could benefit those who are feeling very angry, confused, and depressed to help them cope with life and understand the need to start over, rather than feeling wasted and unable to think for themselves.

The emotional well-being discussed in this work is a crucial aspect that all congregations, including those represented in the study, should consider. It is important to provide support for the mental well-being of ex-religious individuals, similar to how support is offered to divorced partners during and after the process. I understand that this analogy is not entirely parallel because ex-religious individuals are not "divorced" from God. However, they are still separated from their former congregations. Providing them with material support is not sufficient; as Canon Law suggests, support should be holistic and comprehensive, encompassing spiritual and psychological well-being. I am also aware that dismissed religious individuals may reject this offer, especially if they are angry with the process. However, it is important for them to know that the option for emotional healing is available. After examining the trauma experienced by some former religious individuals, it is important for them to embrace a new horizon through therapy, spiritual guidance, or any other means of alleviating their inner pain. This way, life beyond the convent wall can become fulfilling, meaningful, and life-giving.

Chapter Five

Life Beyond Convent Walls and New Horizons

The chapters above have evidenced that many former religious women experience emotional trauma. This emotional distress is either due to the unfavorable nature of the dismissal process or their desire to continue living a religious life. It was discovered that some individuals who left religious life on their own found it a relieving experience and are happy. They have reported feeling a sense of relief after leaving religious life and are either happily married or serving God as lay faithful. However, a significant number of those who were dismissed from religious life have unfortunately experienced feelings of shame, anger, resentment, emptiness, despair, isolation, depression, and a few have even attempted suicide. Some people struggle with life, while others continue to wear religious habits under the guise of belonging to religious institutes.

This is not surprising since dismissing religious persons, in some cultures, is perceived as grave and socially unacceptable, as well as a rejection of the sacrifice offered to God. A participant in Group 3 explained: "Dismissal from religious life is sometimes perceived as bad luck, associated with misfortune which leads to societal rejection." Although married and with two children, ex-religious # 23 is still depressed and not happy. Ex-religious # 16's mother suffered a heart attack when the news was conveyed to her. After spending 19 years in religious life, ex-religious # 2 experienced rejection from her family members, etc. This apparent negative connotation of dismissal from religious life may stem from the sacredness and reverence with which sacrifice to God is valued in some cultures. It suggests that these participants are going through emotional trauma.

Beyond the Pain of Separating from Religious Life

Have you ever noticed that when you board a plane on an overcast, gloomy day, as soon as you fly past the clouds, you are met with the sun and a bright day? The sun is always in the sky during the day, even when it's obscured by clouds. We may not see the sun if we cannot get past the clouds. It's the same with a painful experience: we can't break through the pain of life when we are clouded by it. When the painful separation from religious life clouds your vision and depresses you, it's difficult to break through the cloud of negativity.

I recently watched a 2022 Netflix documentary produced by Jonah Hill. The documentary features his therapist, Phil Stutz, and is titled "Stutz." In the documentary, Phil Stutz discusses his approach to mental health and shares universal tools that can help guide us back to a state of wholeness when we are dealing with pain, shame, rejection, isolation, negative feelings toward ourselves or others, unforgiveness, grudges, bitterness, or injustices inflicted by others.[7]

One of Stutz's tools is active love. When we love ourselves, other people's opinions do not affect us. This doesn't mean we ignore genuine feedback; it just means we don't get stuck in self-pity or negative voices. Have you ever felt trapped in the maze of pain

---

[7] https://www.netflix.com/search?q=Stutz

caused by what people did to you or what they say about you? Many former religious persons are still dealing with the pain caused by leaving their religious life. Love of self means that we are comfortable with our true selves and accept who we are; we are not trapped in the maze of our past mistakes or what people did or did not do to us. At times, we might spend our whole lives trapped and consumed by the betrayal of a friend and try to seek revenge. The solution is not revenge but active love.

Before we can love others, we must first love ourselves. To cultivate this self-love, Stutz suggests the following: Imagine being surrounded by love energy in the universe. Then, gently but firmly, gather all this love energy into your heart. In doing so, you become the primary source of this love. This love brings positive energy and the ability to love oneself. Those who have left religious life could experience freedom from self-blame, self-hate, animosity, and bitterness, as well as the web of pain that can accompany leaving religious life, if they practice active love.

When we have love in our hearts, it's time to share it by actively sending love energy to those we despise, hate, or are angry with. We also send active love to those who cause us pain and we're not ready to forgive, or those we want to exact revenge against. During meditation, imagine sending this positive love energy to these individuals, and you feel active love entering them as you become unified in love with them. Active love liberates us from the entanglement of unforgiveness and bitterness. It's not justifying the actions of the person who has hurt you, but rather about reclaiming your freedom and releasing yourself from anger, unforgiveness, hatred, grudges, and resentments. That is why Jesus tells us: "Love your enemies and pray for those who persecute you that you may be children of your Father in heaven. He causes his sun to rise on the evil and the good and sends rain on the righteous and the unrighteous. If you love those who love you, what reward will you get? What is unusual about that? Do not the tax collectors do the same?" (Mt. 5:44-48). When we can send this active love to others, especially those who cause us pain, healing begins to take place, and we become whole again.

Stutz also mentioned the concept of radical acceptance as another helpful tool. Some individuals who have been dismissed from religious congregations may still be in denial as part of the grieving process, which is why they continue to wear the religious habit associated with their former congregations. Radical acceptance involves acknowledging and embracing your emotions, such as the sorrow of transitioning out of religious life and the desire to find purpose beyond this challenging situation. Instead of denying your feelings and becoming trapped in pain and negativity, ask yourself: "What can I learn from this experience? What other choices or options do I have? What new possibilities or horizons do I want to embrace?" These questions can help you consider different options and opportunities, rather than feeling trapped in a closed chapter of your life.

Another tool by Stutz is the Grateful Flow. This tool helps a heartbroken person to look beyond the pain and imagine what they are thankful for. Gratitude breaks the cloud of negativity and pain by sending positive energy to the heart of the one who is overwhelmed, filling it with optimism. Most of the time, we focus on what we don't have rather than what we do have. We are quick to count our losses but hesitant to count our blessings. When we adopt an attitude of gratitude, it diminishes the toxic and negative energy of unforgiveness, aggression, frustration, regret, hatred, envy, bitterness, resentment, hopelessness, and anger toward ourselves and others. We begin to sleep better, become happier, reduce stress, and lower blood pressure. All the body aches and stomach upsets caused by animosities and grudges will become history. The renowned Roman philosopher Cicero said, "Gratitude is not only the greatest of virtues but the parent of all virtues." Sometimes we get trapped and caught up in life's temporary difficulties, forgetting that life is mostly good. It pays to reflect more deeply on some of these painful experiences and to consider the gifts we have developed through them.

"Certainly, we are the writers of our stories; therefore, we must choose how to handle the sufferings and pains that visit us and cause us heartaches. We could find meaning in every painful experience or get trapped in them. We can see the pain in our lives as learning experiences that make us stronger or as experiences that ruin us. We could allow pain to either inform us or define us! The choice is ours!" (Ogbuji, *My Darling Joe,* 2023). Pain can sometimes lead to unhealthy thoughts, decisions, and actions. It can also cripple us if we let it. Holding onto and replaying painful experiences and animosity can cause "cancer of the heart." In many cases, these painful experiences are opportunities for learning and growth if we look beyond the pain. However, if we focus only on past hurts and closed doors, we may miss out on new opportunities.

"In the face of these difficulties, we can either give up and lose hope or see these obstacles as a stepping stone on our faith journey. It is not as if we will validate evil or forget, but we are not to get stuck in a maze of "I am not good enough," wallow in self-pity, or get trapped in the negative voices in our heads. The key is replacing our negative thoughts with the spirit of thanksgiving. Gratitude has a way of helping us find meaning in life's challenges and suffering. It enables us to maintain a positive outlook on a brighter future, even when it seems bleak. Gratitude sends positive energy to our minds and helps us break the cloud of pain" (Ogbuji, 2023).

Steps to Healing by Stutz

— Recognize that you are hurt. Being aware of our pain is the first step toward healing. When we acknowledge the presence of our pain, we begin to gain power over it. However, if we ignore or deny it, we remain trapped and give it power over us. When emotions such as regret, hate, fear, anger, shame, guilt, and sadness arise, we tend to suppress them; we prefer not to experience them. We often try to bury them and feign indifference. It is better not to push them down. Through awareness, we can identify and name our feelings. For instance: "I feel anxious about the interview." I am frustrated about my homework, which I cannot finish." "I am sad that my friend is moving to another country." "I am humiliated by her actions." The act of naming our feelings allows us to take a pause and use our breath to calm our minds. When we approach emotions and feelings in a neutral manner, they will no longer have a strong impact on us. These emotions are valid and deserve attention.

— When emotions are intense, they can be felt physically in the body as tightness in the chest, digestive problems, difficulty sleeping, inability to concentrate, body aches, ulcers, high blood pressure, and excessive fatigue. The body may also feel stiff and tense. Then you begin to replay the experience with some thoughts: "I cannot imagine this!" "She is so wrong!" "This shouldn't be!" "I am going to make her pay!" "I'm going to let the congregation have it!" Challenge these intense emotions with questions: "Why am I feeling this extreme pain? What need in me is not met? What expectations are not being met? Where am I still stuck? Why am I unable to move past this pain?" Remember that your temporary emotions should not define you. They come and go! Just be patient, and with mindfulness and meditation, reflect and stay with your feelings.

Key to the process

— Don't be too hard on yourself. It is a process that takes time. Don't expect to be healed overnight.

— Recognize the impact of the past experience or past wound on you.

— Let go of the pain and learn to forgive whether the person wants/deserves it or not. It is not about them; it is about you. Embrace the spirit of gratitude, and it will replace your pain with joy, peace, empathy, and hope.

— Talk to your emotions: "I understand that you are hurting! And I am sorry you are hurting. I know deep inside you want to move on and be better!" Self-talk brings positive energy.

— Consciously and in the spirit of gratitude, pray for the one who has hurt you. Use a release prayer and virtualize the release. When you say it, truly believe it!

— Love yourself again. Remind yourself that you are enough!

Life beyond the convent's walls can be stress-free if the person leaving the convent is ready to let go, embrace change, and start a new life. It is said that when one door closes, God opens another door. However, if former religious individuals fixate on closed doors, how can they expect to notice an open door? At times, we focus all our attention on a closed door without discerning the other opportunities God presents to us. We need to peel off the cataract of self-pity that has clouded our eyes, so that we can clearly see the sun shining brightly during the day.

When the door to religious life closes, a person must find a new path toward a different horizon. Moving from a religious community to another vocation is a major change. It is a process and a journey that involves rebuilding one's life and discovering new meaning. It involves letting go of past hurts, nurturing hope for the future, and embracing new experiences, challenges, and opportunities with resilience, even when faced with subconscious fears. This journey represents personal growth, self-discovery, optimism, and a deep desire for renewal. A former religious person may struggle to explore new options if they remain focused on self-pity, a closed door, and a lack of openness to new possibilities.

The mind is powerful! When a person focuses on negative thoughts and self-pity, their actions and reactions tend to be negative as well. This reminds me of a story about a bowl of water. A young boy was torn down by gossip and negative talk from people around him. He went to a wise man and asked how he could focus on his life rather than dwell on negative thoughts or on how others perceive him. The wise man told him to fill a bowl with water and walk around the community, being careful not to spill a single drop. People mocked and laughed at him, but he stayed focused. When he returned, the wise man asked the boy to describe what he saw along the road. The boy replied that he only saw the bowl of water. His focus was on keeping the water from spilling, so he didn't notice the people laughing and mocking him. When we remain focused, we will not let self-pity, negative criticism, or a pessimistic attitude toss us around like a wave.

The insight from Stutz is that while we cannot control the pity zone, we can swiftly escape it by refusing to give it a seat. We will not be perfect or win every time, but we have the unstoppable will to move forward rather than linger in negativity or pain. Our painful experiences are not our lives. They are supposed to inform us, not define us. We can learn from them and move forward. Yes, it hurts! But we must not stay where we have fallen! Jesus did not! He fell three times and got up three times. By the way, pain does not go away entirely because there is no perfect life, relationship, or world, but we keep working on getting better with the pain that we experience in life. It is an illusion to think that there is a perfect life or relationship without pain. No one is immune to pain except for a rare genetic condition! Happiness depends on how we accept this fact and what we do with it. Radical acceptance helps people accept what has happened and seek other options with a positive mindset.

Chapter Six

Recommendations

This chapter outlines recommendations from the four groups interviewed: leaders and formators from diverse congregations, religious sisters without leadership roles, and dismissed members.

Recommendations from Leaders

It's important to exercise patience when dismissing someone from religious life. As leaders, we may feel threatened by individuals with unique personalities and those who are bold enough to challenge us. Therefore, conducting a thorough investigation is crucial before making any hasty decisions that could lead to regret. Rushing into such decisions can have a negative impact on people's livelihoods and their vocation. We must be fair and just, listen to our members, and give them a second chance rather than dismissing them for insignificant reasons.

Former religious individuals require appropriate support. Unfortunately, we often overlook their needs and fail to provide them with adequate assistance, resulting in unnecessary suffering. Sometimes, we show partial support, which is not very charitable. While we may provide some financial assistance, emotional support is often lacking. It's important that we take steps to address these issues. Instead of making fun of their misfortune, we should focus on helping them deal with their situation through counseling and psychological assistance, and monitor their progress as they adapt to life outside the convent.

The Holy Spirit guides the formation process. However, there are times when our lack of information allows tribal sentiments and prejudice to influence our actions, resulting in harm to others. It is crucial to seek adequate knowledge and interact with others with kindness, empathy, compassion, and sensitivity.

It's our responsibility to be transparent and honest about the reasons for a candidate's separation from a congregation. This information should be communicated early on during the initial formation process. If there is any uncertainty or doubt, it's our duty to dismiss the candidate sooner rather than later, ensuring a clear and honest process.

Dismissing a member can be one of the most challenging decisions a leader faces. It is recommended that Canon Law be applied during this process. To ensure fairness, it is essential to give several warnings to the person so they are aware of their actions and have the opportunity to improve. Instead of dismissing members who have spent over ten years in religious life, let us explore alternative disciplinary measures.

At times, the leadership team may not agree with each other, leading to disunity, hatred, bias, prejudice, and a desire for revenge. While some members may be rightfully dismissed, others may not. It's important to avoid jealousy, listen to all sides of the story, seek clarification, and embrace a participatory leadership style rather than one based on tribal affiliations.

Some individuals join religious life with dented motives, such as gaining education, security, shelter, and prestige. Therefore, it is crucial to purify their motivations before starting the formation process. At the beginning of the formation process, offering counseling sessions can help individuals from troubled and violent family backgrounds to work through their past experiences, helping them to live a mature religious life.

Recommendations from Formators

The experience of being dismissed from a formation house can be very painful and requires a lot of prayer, patience, and time to heal. It's important for us, formators, to handle the situation with great care, respect, and deep listening, without any prejudice or bias. Unfortunately, some formators may act as if they have ultimate authority and intimidate formees with threats of dismissal, leading formandis to hide their true selves. This creates an environment in which formees feel like their survival in the formation process depends solely on their ability to comply with the formator's expectations.

It's important to provide psychological and financial support for individuals who leave religious life to help them adjust to their new lifestyle. Currently, we are not doing enough in these areas. Many individuals may experience social rejection, so it's crucial to provide both psychological support and financial assistance. We need to create a policy to support former members, ensuring they receive fair and equal financial and emotional support. It's important to avoid dismissing perpetually professed members and instead consider alternative disciplinary actions, using dismissal only as a last resort.

During the process of forming individuals, personal issues may arise that could lead to countertransference. As formators, it is important to address our own issues by seeking guidance from professionals such as counselors and spiritual directors, rather than projecting them onto the formandis. We must exercise patience and remember that each person has their own unique calling. We must respect differences and individuality and listen without bias or judgment. It is also important to give people a second chance and use dismissal as the last resort after all other options have been exhausted.

Formators have a responsibility to assist their formandis in their personal growth by identifying their areas for growth and improvement. If there are doubts about a formee's suitability, it is better to release them early rather than wait until they have spent many years as temporal professed members only to be dismissed when it is time to make perpetual vows.

Recommendations from Religious Members without Leadership Roles

We need transparency and fairness for all members during the dismissal process. It's important to have a consistent approach to treating dismissed members rather than using different measures depending on who is in power. In other words, it is important to develop a plan on how dismissed members should be treated and supported, giving them a second chance, an opportunity to defend themselves, and using dismissal sparingly.

We should provide sufficient support to former members so they can adjust quickly, not only financially but also emotionally, psychologically, and spiritually. Proper dialogue with their family members is important, too.

We need to send only mature and trained formators to the formation ministry so that individuals can be formed to be responsible religious, thereby preventing the deformation of members. Formation is the work of the Holy Spirit. We should allow the Spirit of God to lead the process and help us treat people with respect. The formation process should be free so that those being formed will not feel the need to wear masks to hide their true selves, only to reveal their true colors when they make their perpetual profession. If there are doubts about a member, we should learn to dismiss them as early as possible rather than waiting until they are much older.

Leaders should ensure that members' evaluations are fair and unbiased. It is essential for leaders to listen to all parties involved and remain open to the truth, rather than relying solely on the opinions of formators. It would be helpful to establish a confidential mechanism for formators' evaluation so that formees can share their experiences with the appropriate authorities. When formators know that they are also being assessed, they are likely to be more mindful of how they treat those they are forming. Additionally, having a formation team to oversee formators' conduct is important to prevent abuse of power.

Recommendations from Discontinued Religious Persons

During the dismissal process, congregations should follow Canon Law procedures, provide warnings, and avoid bias and injustice. Leaders should be fair and just in their dealings with members and foster a culture of open communication. It's important for both parties to engage in empathetic listening and to give people a second chance rather than dismissing them as the first course of action.

Formators should learn to listen to and understand different personalities. They should be patient with the formation process and accept formees/formandis who differ from them. Formators should stop keeping records of malice and forgive from their hearts.

Congregations should have a standardized plan and structure for handling dismissed members, ensuring that all are treated equally. Former members should be provided with psychological, emotional, spiritual, and financial support. Bishops should ensure that congregations follow the appropriate process outlined in Canon Law when dismissing members, rather than doing so out of malice, tribal sentiments, or unfounded rumors. It's essential to support former members as they transition to life outside the religious community. Today's society does not always support those who have left religious life, so it's important to help them heal and adjust quickly. Once in a while, it is also important to have a follow-up plan to ensure the welfare of the dismissed individuals even after the process is over.

Leaders should send trained, morally upright members who are compassionate and empathetic listeners to the formation ministry. Additionally, leaders should hold annual confidential meetings to evaluate the formators, as many of the individuals they are forming live in fear. Sometimes, sisters in initial formation are not respected; they are treated as second-class citizens because they have not yet made their perpetual vows. Everyone, regardless of their stage of formation, deserves respect.

Sisters in the initial formation should be allowed and encouraged to be themselves rather than wear masks just to please the formator. Formators should suggest areas for growth to those in the formation process rather than waiting until the evaluation period to use these areas against them. When there is uncertainty about a formee's eligibility for a specific congregation, it is crucial to assist them in deciding to leave religious life so they can pursue other vocations.

Summary

- There is a need for pastoral care, spiritual direction, and therapy: The church needs to invest time and energy into equipping former religious persons. As more women enter convents, more will discern out, leading to a greater need for care and support.
- Peer support group therapy among ex-religious is vital.
- Over 80% of those who participated in this research work recommended that each congregation develop a policy regarding adequate and uniform spiritual, psychological, emotional, and financial support of the members who leave the congregation. This policy is essential so that each member who left a

congregation at a particular stage and age will benefit from the same measure.

— The majority of the participants also suggested psychological training and formation of formators so they would be well-equipped for the work of formation.

— A good number of formees who join religious life come from broken homes, so it is necessary to help them through the counseling process at the initial stages of formation so that the formation process will help them to grow.

— Also recommended was being patient with a member's dismissal process, allowing room for dialogue, gathering adequate information, praying for the guidance of the Holy Spirit, and using a proper discernment process as explained in the constitutions of every congregation/institute to avoid unfounded information, bias, and tribal sentiment. It is also recommended that warnings be given as recorded in the Canon Law and dismissal be used as a last resort (Can. 1341, 1348, 1733).

— There is a need to educate parents and candidates that formation is a process of discerning God's will to avoid a false hope that everyone who joins a convent must become a nun/sister. Thus, discernment is a journey, and dismissed members are not sinners. They have only discovered the will of God and wish to try another vocation. Every vocation is a gift and beautiful!

— Each congregation to have a social support group for all the ex-members, where they will gather at least biannually to share, support, and ritualize their life experiences as former members.

— The Church should strive to better understand and support former religious persons by providing necessary resources and assistance. If necessary, priests should include it in their homily.

Conclusion

The data presented highlights the fear and concern regarding the emotional trauma experienced by individuals who have left religious communities. Participants agreed on the importance of providing therapy and counseling to support healing, as the effects of leaving religious life can persist until individuals adjust to life outside the convent. It appears that many participants agreed that leaders should have more information before deciding to dismiss someone and should also follow proper procedures during the dismissal process.

Additionally, it was emphasized that it is very important to send adequately trained formators to religious formation houses. This work demonstrates that unjust dismissal from religious life can have a profound impact on an ex-member. Participants stressed the importance of approaching the process with patience, compassion, prayer, dialogue, adequate information, and proper discernment, rather than resorting to unfounded rumors and gossip. To this end, Pope Francis emphasizes, "I would ask you to think about my frequent comments about criticism, gossip, envy, jealousy, and hostility as ways of acting that have no place in our communities. This being the case, the path of charity open before us is almost infinite since it entails mutual acceptance and concern, practicing a communion of goods, both material and spiritual, fraternal correction, and respect for those who are weak ... it is the "mystique of living together" which makes our life "a sacred pilgrimage."

The traumatic feelings that often occur immediately following the separation or dismissal of a religious member from a consecrated institute can be overwhelming. Such feelings can cause the ex-members to experience bursts of aggressive behavior and irritability toward those around them, such as the Church, their former congregation members, and family members, as well as themselves, as a result of guilt, shame, self-pity, or self-blame. This work discovered that such individuals suffer from depression, insomnia, low self-image, constant anger, rejection, and a feeling of hopelessness, as well as the contemplation of suicide. Some affected individuals who participated in this work are pretty depressed, troubled, agitated, confused, and live a chaotic life that sometimes exceeds their ability to cope with life-challenging issues.

These individuals must be supported through therapy or spiritual direction to facilitate their healing process. The ex-religious will also find alternative ways to think positively about the dismissal process to avoid being dragged back with negative thoughts. Because the dismissed religious go through religious trauma, therapy might empower them to cope with life after leaving religious life. Cognitive therapy can help an ex-religious person think more positively about life. For instance, rather than thinking: "The leaders used a demeaning method to dismiss me, that is why I cannot function well in society. Or I am ashamed to face the reality." The person can change the negative attitude to: "Maybe I need to get up and accept that there is a better life outside the walls of the convent." Consequently, rather than wearing religious habits and pretending to be religious, the individual can accept the reality of not belonging to a religious institute, face it with a positive attitude and courage, quit living in denial, and acquire constructive coping strategies.

In his Post-Synodal Apostolic Exhortation, Vita Consecrata (1996), Pope St. John Paul II explained, "You have not only a glorious history to remember and to recount, but also a great history still to be accomplished! Look to the future, where the Spirit is sending you in order to do even greater things" (# 110). Similarly, Pope Francis, in his 2014 Apostolic Letter to all Consecrated People, on the occasion of the Year of Consecrated Life, encouraged all consecrated people to look to the past with gratitude, live the present with passion, and embrace the future with hope.

It is impossible to look to the future with hope while being stuck in the past. No one can remain in self-pity and expect new results. Therapy, spiritual guidance, and support from friends and family members can significantly help individuals navigate their challenges and embrace new beginnings. They provide a supportive environment for self-exploration, healthier coping mechanisms, emotional well-being, and personal growth for better relationships with themselves, God, and others.

References

American Psychiatric Association. (2022). *Diagnostic and Statistical Manual of Mental Disorders*, 5th Ed Text Revision. Washington, DC: American Psychiatric Publishing.

Auerbach, C. F., & Silverstein, L. B. (2003). *Qualitative Data: An Introduction to Coding and Analysis.* New York: New York University Press.

Babbie, E., (2008). *The Basics of Social Research.* 4th Edition. Belmont, CA: Thomson Higher Education.

Banyard, P., & Flanagan, C. (2009). *Ethical Issues & Guidelines in Psychology.* New York: Routledge.

Barra, D., Carlson, E., & Maize, M. (1993). The Dark Night of the Spirit: Grief Following a Loss in Religious Identity. In K. Doka & J. Morgan (Eds.), *Death and Spirituality.* Amityville, NY: Baywood.

Beck, A. T. (1967). *Depression: Causes and Treatment.* Philadelphia: University of Pennsylvania Press.

Beck, A. T., & Steer, R. A. (1993). Beck Anxiety Inventory Manual. San Antonio: Harcourt Brace and Company.

Beck, A. T., Epstein, N., & Harrison, R. (1983). Cognitions, Attitudes, and Personality Dimensions In Depression. *British Journal of Cognitive Psychotherapy.*

Beck, J. S. (2011). *Cognitive Behavioural Therapy: Basics and Beyond*, (2nd Ed.). New York: Guilford Press.

Becker, D. M. (2001). Integrating Behavioural and Social Sciences with Public Health. In N. Schneiderman, M. A. Speers, J. M. Silvia, H. Tomes & J. H. Gentry (Eds.), *Public Health and Religion* (pp. 351-368). Washington, DC: American Psychological Association.

Beitel, M., Genova, M., Schuman-Olivier, Z., Arnold, R., Avants, S. K., & Margolin, A. (2007). Reflections by inner-city drug users on a Buddhist-based spirituality-focused therapy: A qualitative study. *American Journal of Orthopsychiatry*, 77(1), 1–9. https://doi.org/10.1037/0002-9432.77.1.1

Benjamin Jr, L. T., DeLeon, P. H., Freedheim, D. K., & VandenBos, G. R. (2003). Psychology as a Profession. In Donald K. Freedheim & Irving B. Weiner (Eds), *Handbook of Psychology* Vol. 1,

History of Psychology. (pp. 27-46). New Jersey: John Wiley & Sons, Inc.

Berger, P. L. (1990). *The Sacred Canopy*. New York: Anchor Books.

Bierman, A. (2005). The Effects of Childhood Maltreatment on Adult Religiosity and Spirituality: Rejecting God the Father Because of Abusive Fathers? *Journal of the Scientific Study of Religion*, 44 (3), pp. 349-359.

Blanchette, M. C., & Maloney, R. P. (2009). A guide for religious beginning spiritual direction. *Review for Religious*, 68(1), 80–87.

Blaxter, L., Hughes, C. & Tight, M. (2006). *How to Research*. 3rd Edition. New York: Open University Press.

Blocher, D. H. (2000). *The Evolution of Counselling Psychology*. New York: Springer Publishing Company.

Butler, A. C., & Beck, J. S. (2000). Cognitive Therapy Outcomes: A Review of MetaAnalyses. *Journal of the Norwegian Psychological Association*, 37, 1-9.

Canon Law Society of America. (1983). *Code of Canon Law: Latin-English Edition*. Washington, D.C. Libreria Editrice Vaticana.

Catechism of the Catholic Church (2011). *Wayback Machine.* http://www.vatican.va/archive/ENG0015/__P2A.HTM.

Chen, Y. Y., & Koenig, H. G. (2006). Traumatic Stress and Religion: Is there a Relationship? A Review of Empirical Findings. *Journal of Religion and Health*, 10, 1-11.

Collins, R. M. (2017). *Called By God: Discernment and Preparation for Religious Life.* Steubenville, OH: Emmaus Road Publishing.

Corey, G. (2015). *Theory and Practice of Counselling and Psychotherapy*, (10th Ed). Belmont, CA: Cengage Learning.

Craig, R. J. (2005). *Clinical & Diagnostic Interviewing*, 2nd Edition. New York: Rowman & Littlefield Publishers, Inc.

Daly, R. M. (2020). Pastoral Care of Women Who Have Left the Convent. *Homiletic and Pastoral Review Magazine.* https://www.hprweb.com/2020/01/pastoralcare-ofwomen-whohave-left-the-convent/

Davidson, P. (2007). Psychology as Philosophy. In Jose Luis Bermudez (Ed.) *Philosophy of Psychology: Contemporary Readings*, (pp. 22-30). New York: Routledge.

Davis, R. (2016). Journeying Through Physical Health. In Barbara Douglas, Ray Woolfe, Sheelagh Strawbridge, Elaine Kasket & Victoria Galbraith, (Eds.) *The Handbook of Counselling Psychology*, 4th Edition (pp. 479-495). Thousand Oaks, CA: Sage Publications.

Dawson, C. (2002). *Practical Research Methods: A UserFriendly Guide to Mastering Research Techniques and Projects.* United Kingdom: Howtobooks.

De Lame, D. (2010). Grey Nairobi: Sketches of Urban Socialites. In Helen ChartonBigot & Deyssi RodriguezTorres (Eds.) *Nairobi Today: A Paradox of a Fragmented City* (pp. 167-214). Dar es Salam, Tanzania: Mkuki na Nyota Publishers.

Despres, R. (2017). Six Signs and Symptoms of Psychological Trauma. *Active Beat.* http://www.activebeat.com/yourhealth/6-signsand-symptomsof-psychologicaltrauma/.

Dowd, E. T. (2002). History and Recent Development in Cognitive Psychotherapy. In Leahy R. L., and Dowd E. T. (Eds), *Clinical Advances in Cognitive Psychotherapy: Theory and Application* (15-28). New York: Springer Publishing Company.

Dwight, J. H. (2005). Seasons of Change: Adjustment Disorder as Summons to Life Structure. In Sharon G. Mijares & Gurucharan S. Khalsa (Eds.) T*he Psychospiritual Clinician's Handbook: Alternative Methods for Understanding and Treating Mental Disorders*, (33-50). New York: Haworth Press, Inc.

Elkins, D. N. (2009). *Humanistic Psychology: A Clinical Manifesto: A Critique of Clinical Psychology and the Need for Progressive Alternatives.* Colorado Springs, CO: University of Rockies Press.

Ellis, A. (1957). Rational Psychotherapy and Individual Psychology. *Journal of Individual Psychology*, 13: 38-44.

Ellis, A. (1989). The History of Cognition in Psychotherapy. In Arkowitz, H., Beutler, L. E., & Simon, K. (Eds.) *Comprehensive Handbook of Cognitive Therapy*, (1-14). New York: Plenum Press.

Ellis, A. (2001). *Overcoming Destructive Beliefs, Feelings, and Behaviours: New Directions for Rational Emotive Behaviour Therapy*. Prometheus Books.

Ellis, A., Abrams, M., & Abrams, L. D. (2009). *Personality Theories: Critical Perspectives*. Thousand Oaks, CA: Sage Publication. Encyclopedia.com. Beck, Aaron Temkin. www.encyclopedia.com/article-1G2-3456300014/beckaaron-temkin.html

Erikson, E. H. (1950). *Childhood and society*. New York: Norton.

Erikson, E. H. (1959) *Identity and the Life Cycle*. New York: International Universities Press.

Erskine, R. G. & Moursund, J. P. (2011). *Integrative Psychotherapy in Action*. London: Karnao Books Ltd.

Eysenck, M. C. (2004). *Psychology: An International Perspective*. New York: Psychology Press.

Ezeani, C. C. (2007). *Rooted in Christ: Insights into Contemporary Religious and Priestly Formation*. Nigeria: The Ambassador Publications.

Ezeani, C. C. (2017). When You Leave Religious Life, What Then? Accompanying Persons in the Process of Discontinuation from Religious Formation. UISG *Bulletin*, no. 162. www.internationalunionsuperiorsgeneral.org/leavereligious-life/. (This article was also published in *Religious Life Review*, Vol. 55, no. 300, Sept. 2016).

Feltham, C. (1995). *What is Counselling? The Promise and the Problem of the Talking Therapies*. London: Sage Publications.

Ferster, C. B. (1973). "Positive Reinforcement and Behaviour Deficits." In S. A. Winter & E. Cox, (Eds), *Behaviour Modification Techniques for the Special Educators*, (pp.137-156). New York: Arno Press.

Fontana, A. & Rosenheck, R (2004). *Trauma, Change in Strength of Religious Faith, and Mental Health Service Use among Veterans Treated for PTSD*. Journal of Nervous and Mental Disease, 192, 579–584.

Ford-Martin, P. (2001). Sigmund Freud. In Bonnie B. Strickland (Ed.), *The Gale Encyclopaedia of Psychology* (p. 261), 2nd Edition. Detroit, MI: Gale Group.

Freud, S. (1914). On Narcissism: An Introduction. *Standard Edition*, 14, 73–102. -- (1915).

Thoughts for the Times on War and Death. *Standard Edition*, 14, 275–300. -- (1916). On Transience. *Standard Edition*, 14, 305–307. -- (1917). Mourning and Melancholia. *Standard Edition*, 14, 243–258. -- (1923). The Ego and the Id. *Standard Edition*, 19, 12–66.

Fuchs, A. H., & Milar K. S. (2003). "Psychology as a Science." In D. K. Freedheim & I. B. Weiner (Eds), *Handbook of Psychology* Vol. 1, *History of Psychology*. (pp. 1-26). New Jersey: John Wiley & Sons, Inc.

Gitau, M. (2016). "Formation of Consecrated Persons in East Africa: Contexts, Struggles, and Possibilities." In *Consecrated Life in Africa: Yesterday, Today and Tomorrow*, (pp. 125-141). A symposium organized by Tangaza University College, Nairobi, from 23-26th September, 2015. Nairobi, Kenya: Paulines Publications Africa.

Glaser, D. (2002). Emotional Abuse and Neglect (Psychological Maltreatment): A Conceptual Framework. *Child Abuse & Neglect*, 26, 697-714.

Goodman, M. L., Grouls, A., Chen, C. X., Keiser, P. H., & Gitari, S. (2016). Adverse Childhood Experiences Predict Alcohol Consumption Patterns among Kenyan Mothers. *Substance Use & Misuse Journal.* Vol. 52, (5), 632-638.

Greence, R. R. (2010). *Human Behaviour: Theory and Social Work Practice*, 3rd Edition. London, UK: Aldine Transaction Publishers.

Grogan, J. L. (2008). *A Cultural History of the Humanistic Psychology Movement in America.* Ann Arbor, MI: ProQuest LLC.

Halvachizadeh, S., Mariani, D., & Pfeifer, R. (2025). Impact of trauma on society. *European Journal of Trauma and Emergency Surgery*, 51(1), 155. https://doi.org/10.1007/s00068-025-02824-8

Henton, W. W., & Iversen I. H. (2012). *Classical Conditioning and Operant Conditioning: A Response Pattern Analysis.* New York: SpringerVerlag.

Ibrahim, F. A. (1985). Effective CrossCultural Counselling and Psychotherapy. *The Journal of Counselling Psychologist,* 13, 625-638.

Jeenah, F. Y., & Moosa, M. Y. (2017). The Impact of Trauma on the Psyche. In G. C. Velmahos, E. Degiannis, & D. Doll, (Eds.), *Penetrating Trauma: A Practical Guide on Operative Technique and PeriOperative Management*, (pp.581-588), 2nd Edition. Berlin: SpringerVerlag.

Johnson, A. (2014). Kenya: Geography, Culture, and Economics. *Borgen Magazine*, January Edition. https://www.borgenmagazine.com/kenyageography-cultureeconomics.

Kenya Conference of Catholic Bishops. (2014). *Guidelines to Safeguard Aspects of Consecrated Life in Kenya.* Nairobi, Kenya: Paulines Publication Africa.

Kersting, K. (2003). Religion and Spirituality in the Treatment Room. Monitor on Psychology, 34 (11), 40.

Kiaziku, V. C. (2007). *Consecrated Life in Bantu Africa.* Nairobi, Kenya: Paulines Publications Africa.

Koenig, H. G., George, L. K., & Titus, P. (2004). Religion Spirituality and Health in Medically Ill Hospitalized Older Patients. *Journal of the American Geriatrics Society*, 52, 554-562.

Krapp, K. M. (2004). A Study Guide for Psychologists and Their Theories for Students: Aaron Temkin Beck. Farmington, MI: Cengage Learning.

Kvale, S., & Brinkmann, S. (2009). *Interviews: Learning the Craft of Qualitative Research Interviewing.* 2nd Ed. Thousand Oaks, CA: Sage Publications.

Lauver, P. J. (1986). Extending Counselling Cross-Culturally: Invisible Barriers. A paper presented at the annual meeting of the California Association for Counselling and Development. San Francisco, CA: ED 274937.

Leahy, R. (2003). *Cognitive Therapy Techniques: A Practitioner's Guide*. New York: The Guilford Press.

Lewis-Morrarty, E., Degnan, K. A., Chronis-Tuscano, A., Pine, D. S., Henderson, H. A., & Fox, N. A. (2015). Infant Attachment Security and Early Childhood Behavioural Inhibition Interact to Predict Adolescent Social Anxiety Symptoms. *Child Development*, 86, Issue 2, 598–613.

Lezohupski, R. (2016). "Juridical Considerations in the Dismissal of Religious in the African Context." In *Consecrated Life in Africa: Yesterday, Today and Tomorrow*, (pp. 99-111). A symposium was organized by Tangaza University College, Nairobi, from 23-26th September 2015. Nairobi, Kenya: Paulines Publications Africa.

Lindridge, A. (2008). Spirituality Matters. *Mental Health Today*, 30-33. http://www.ncbi.nlm.nih.gov/pubmed/18165982.

Maganya, I. (2016). "Doing Formation in East Africa." In *Consecrated Life in Africa: Yesterday, Today and Tomorrow*, (pp. 141-146). A Symposium organized by Tangaza University College, Nairobi, from 23-26th September 2015. Nairobi, Kenya: Paulines Publications Africa.

Mahoney, M. J. (1974). *Cognition and Behaviour Modification*. Cambridge, MA: Ballinger.

Marshall, C., & Rossman, G., (2011). *Designing Qualitative Research*. 5th Edition. Thousand Oaks, CA: Sage Publications.

McLeod, S. A. (2015). Cognitive Behavioural Therapy. www.simplypsychology.org/cognitivetherapy.html.

Mijares, S. G., & Khalsa, G. S. (2005). Introduction. In Sharon G. Mijares & Gurucharan S. Khalsa (Eds.) *The Psychospiritual Clinician's Handbook: Alternative Methods for Understanding and*

Treating Mental Disorders, (1-12). New York: Haworth Press, Inc.

Miltenberger, R. G. (2012). *Behaviour Modification: Principles and Procedures*, 5th Edition. Belmont, CA: Wadsworth Cengage Learning.

Mohr, W. K. (2006). Spiritual Issues in Psychiatric Care. *Perspectives in Psychiatric Care*, 42(3), 174-183.

Muñoz, J. C. (2015). "The Impact of Leaving the Convent on a Woman's Perceived Relationship with God as Viewed Through the Lenses of Attachment and Divorce." PhD Dissertation Published by the Institute for the Psychological Sciences. Now Divine Mercy University, Sterling, Virginia.

Murphy, D. (2017). Introduction to the Textbook on Counselling Psychology. In David Murphy (ed.) *Counselling Psychology: A Textbook for Study and Practice*, (pp. 3-7). Nottingham, UK: British Psychology Society and John Wiley & Sons Ltd.

Myers, J. E., & Sweeney, T. J. (2008). Wellness Counselling: The Evidence Base for Practice. *Journal of Counselling and Development*, 86, 482-493.

Nakato, N. (2016). Implementing Juridical Considerations in the Dismissal of Religious. In *Consecrated Life in Africa: Yesterday, Today and Tomorrow*, (pp. 112-121). A Symposium organized by Tangaza University College, Nairobi, from 23-26th September 2015. Nairobi, Kenya: Paulines Publications Africa.

Nelson, J. M. (2009). *Psychology, Religion, and Spirituality*, New York: Springer.

Netflix Movies. (2022). *Stutz.* https://www.netflix.com/search?q=Stutz

Neukrug, E. S. (2011). *Counselling Theory and Practice.* Belmont, CA: Brooks/Cole Cengage Learning.

Ogbuji, A. H. (2023). *My Darling Joe: A Reflection on a Personal Relationship with Saint Joseph.* St. Louis, MO: En Route Books.

Ogbuji, A. H. (2024). *Influence of Childhood Experiences on Faith Development: A Journey Toward Wholeness.* St. Louis, MO: En Route Books.

Oladeji, B. D., Makanjuola, V. A., & Gureje, O. (2010). "FamilyRelated Adverse Childhood Experiences as Risk Factors for Psychiatric Disorders in Nigeria." *The British Journal of Psychiatry.* 196(3): 186–191.

O'Donohue, W. T. & Fisher, J. E. (2012). The Core Principles of Cognitive Behaviour Therapy. In William T. O'Donohue & Jane E. Fisher (editors) *Cognitive Behaviour Therapy: Core Principles for Practice*, (pp. 1-15). Hoboken, NJ: John Wiley & Sons, Inc.

O'Reilly, L. (2013). *The Impact of Vatican II on Women Religious: Case Study of the Union of Irish Presentation Sisters.* United Kingdom: Cambridge Scholars Publishing.

O'Reilly, M. L. (2004). Spirituality and Mental Health Clients. *Journal of Psychosocial Nursing and Mental Health Services*, 42(7), 44-53.

Pargament, K. I. (1997). *The Psychology of Religion and Coping: Theory, Research and Practice.* New York: Guilford Press.

Pastorino, E. E., & DoylePortillo, S. M. (2012). *What Is Psychology?* 3rd Ed. Belmont, CA: Wadsworth Cengage Learning.

Pastorino, E. E., & DoylePortillo, S. M. (2014). *What Is Psychology?* Foundations, Applications and Integration. Boston, MA: Cengage Learning.

Persons, J. B., & Miranda, J. (2002). Treating Dysfunctional Beliefs: Implications of the MoodState Hypothesis. In Leahy R. L., & Dowd E. T. (Eds), *Clinical Advances in Cognitive Psychotherapy: Theory and Application* (pp. 62-74). New York: Springer Publishing Company.

Piedmont, R. (2007). CrossCultural Generalizability of the Spiritual Transcendence Scale to the Philippines: Spirituality as a Human Universal. *Mental Health, Religion and Culture*, 10, 89-107.

Plock, S. D. (2017). Philosophical Issues in Counselling Psychology. In David Murphy (Ed.), *Counselling Psychology: A Textbook for Study and Practice*, (pp. 36-52). Nottingham, UK: British Psychology Society and John Wiley and Sons Ltd.

Pope Francis. (2014). Apostolic Letter to all Consecrated People, On the Occasion of the Year of Consecrated Life. https://www.vatican.va/content/francesco/en/apost_letters/documents/papafrancesco_letteraap_20141121_lettera-consacrati.html

Pope Francis. (2014). Meeting with the Religious Communities of Korea on the Occasion of the 6th Asian Youth Day from 13-18 August 2014. https://www.vatican.va/content/francesco/en/speeches/2014/august/documents/papafrancesco_20140816_coreacomunita-religiose.html

Pope Francis. (2015). Pope Francis' Address to Formators of Consecrated Men and Women, *Zenit*, April 2015. https://zenit.org/articles/pope-francis-addressto-formatorsof-consecratedmen-andwomen/.

Pope Francis. (2024). *Dilexit Nos: On the Human and Divine Love of the Heart of Jesus Christ.* https://www.vatican.va/content/francesco/en/encyclicals/documents/20241024-enciclicadilexit-nos.html

Pope John Paul II (1996). PostSynodal Apostolic Exhortation Vita Consecrata. https://www.vatican.va/content/johnpaul-ii/en/apost_exhortations/documents/hf_jpii_exh_25031996_vita-consecrata.html

Reeves, A. (2013). *An Introduction to Counselling and Psychotherapy: From Theory to Practice.* London: Sage Publications.

Rogers, C. (1959). A Theory of Therapy, Personality and Interpersonal Relationships as Developed in the ClientCentered Framework. In S. Koch, (Ed.), *Psychology: A Study of a Science.* Vol. 3: *Formulations of the person and the social context.* New York: McGraw Hill.

Russell, J., Jarvis, M., Roberts, C., Dwyer, D., & Putwain, D. (2003). *Angles on Applied Psychology.* United Kingdom: Nelson Thomas Ltd.

Scheck, S. (2005). *Stages of Psychosocial Development According to Erik H. Erikson.* Germany: Grin Verlag.

Schermer, V. L. (2003). *Spirit and Psyche: A New Paradigm for Psychology, Psychoanalysis, and Psychotherapy.* New York: Jessica Kingsley Publishers.

Schneiders, S. M. (2013). *Buying the Field: Catholic Religious Life in Mission to the World: Religious Life in a New Millennium*, Vol. 3. Mahwah, NJ: Paulist Press.

Schnurr, P. P., & Green, B. L. (2004). *Trauma and Health: Physical Health Consequences of Exposure to Extreme Stress.* Washington, DC: American Psychological Association.

Second Vatican Council. (1964). *Lumen Gentium: Dogmatic Constitution on the Church.* https://www.ewtn.com/library/councils/v2church.htm.

Seligman, L., & Reichenberg, L. W. (2014). *Theories of Counselling and Psychotherapy: Systems, Strategies & Skills*, 4th Edition. New Jersey: Upper Saddle River.

Shafranske, E. P. (1991). *Beyond Countertransference: On Being Struck by Faith, Doubt and Emptiness.* American Psychological Association, New Orleans, LA.

Shafranske, E. P., & Sperry, L. (2005). Addressing the Spiritual Dimension in Psychotherapy: Introduction and Overview. In L. Sperry & E. P. Shafranske (Eds.), *Spiritually-Oriented Psychotherapy* (pp. 11-29). Washington, DC: American Psychological Association.

Shamekia, T. (2016) Aaron Beck & Cognitive Therapy: Theory and Concept. Study.com/academy/lesson/aaronbeck-cognitivetherapy-theorylesson-quiz.html.

Smith, R. B. (2017). Divorced from Religious Life. *The Catholic World Report*, Dispatch no. 24. www.catholicworldreport.com/2017/08/10/divorcedfrom-religiouslife/.

Sommers-Flanagan, J. & Sommers-Flanagan R. (2012). *Counselling & Psychotherapy Theories in Context and Practice: Skills, Strategies and Techniques*, 2nd Ed. New Jersey: John Wiley & Sons.

Sorrentino, C. M. (2022). *Behind the Convent Walls: Lifting the Veil of Abuse.* Missio Dei. https://www.missiodeicatholic.org/p/behindthe-conventwalls

Sorrentino, C. M. (2023). *Helping Former Nuns Transition Back into the World.* Catholic Exchange. https://catholicexchange.com/helping-former-nunstransition-backinto-theworld/

St. Ignatius. (2002). *The Companion to the Catechism of the Catholic Church: A Compendium of Texts Referred to in the Catechism of the Catholic Church*, 2nd Ed. San Francisco: Ignatius Press.

Strauss, A. L., & Corbin, J. (1998). *Basics of Qualitative Research: Grounded Theory Procedures and Techniques.* 2nd Edition. Thousand Oaks, CA: Sage Publications.

Szymanska, K., & Palmer, S. (2000). Cognitive Counselling and Psychotherapy. In Palmer S. (Ed), *Introduction to Counselling and Psychotherapy: The Essential Guide* (pp. 56-69). London: Sage Publications.

Taylor, S. E. (2012). "Trend and Befriend Theory." In P. M. Van Lange, A. W. Kruglanski, & E. T. Higgins, (Eds), *Handbook of Theories of Social Psychology*, (Vol.1, pp. 32-49). Thousand Oaks, CA: Sage.

Teyber, E. (2005). *Interpersonal Process in Therapy: An Integrated Model.* Pacific Grove, CA: Brooks Cole Publishers.

The Kenya Catholic Secretariat. (2006). The Kenya Catholic Directory. Nairobi: Kenya: KCD Datacentre.

Vatican II Document. (2014). *Perfectae Caritatis: Decree on the Upto-Date Renewal of Religious Life: A*

Completely Revised Translation in Inclusive Language, edited by Austin Flannery. Collegeville, MN: Liturgical Press.

Wald, K. D., & CalhounBrown, A. (2007). *Religion and Politics in the United States*, 5th Edition. Lanham, MD: Rowman & Littlefield Publishers, Inc.

Weakley, M. A. (2014). *Monastery to Matrimony: A Woman's Journey*. Bloomington, IN: Balboa Press.

Weishaar, M. (2002). Prologue: The Life of Aaron T. Beck. In R. L. Leahy & E. T. Dowd (Eds), *Clinical Advances in Cognitive Psychotherapy: Theory and Application* (pp. 1-14). New York: Springer Publishing Company.

Whitfield, G., & Davidson, A. (2007). *Cognitive Behavioural Theology Therapy*. New York: Radcliffe Publisher.

Wilkins, P. (2010). *Person-Centered Therapy: 100 Key Points*. New York: Routledge.

Winell, M. (2007). *Leaving the Fold: A Guide for Former Fundamentalists and Others Leaving their Religion*. Berkeley, CA: The Apocryphile Press.

Winell, M. (2012). Recovery from Harmful Religion: Religious Trauma Syndrome. http://marlenewinell.net.

Winell, M. (2017). *Understanding Religious Trauma Syndrome: It's Time to Recognize It. British Association for Behavioural and Cognitive Therapies.* http://www.babcp.com/Review/RTSTrauma-fromLeaving-Religion.aspx.

Young, J. S., & Cashwell, C. S. (2011). Integrating Spirituality and Religion in Counselling: An Introduction. In C. S. Cashwell & J. S. Young (Eds.) *Integrating Spirituality and Religion into Counselling: A Guide to Competent Practice*, 2nd Edition, (pp. 1-44). Alexandria, VA: John Wiley & Sons Inc.

Zinnbauer, B. J., Pargament, K. I., & Cowell, B. (1997). Religion and Spirituality: Unfuzzing the Fuzzy. *Journal for the Scientific Study of Religion*, 36, 549-564.

Zoundi, J. (2016). *Dismissal from Consecrated Life. In Consecrated Life in Africa: Yesterday, Today and Tomorrow*, (pp. 119-124). A Symposium organized by Tangaza University College, Nairobi, from 23rd-26th September 2015. Nairobi, Kenya: Paulines Publications.

www.ingramcontent.com/pod-product-compliance
Lightning Source LLC
LaVergne TN
LVHW040220110826
845146LV00005B/1354

9798888705407